Early Islam and Zoroastrian Customs

Alvin R. Poole

Abstract

This book delves into the historical evolution of women's rights within the context of Islam, focusing on the period following the rise of the faith during Mohammad's lifetime. While initially witnessing the establishment of certain women's rights, these advancements faced a decline in the aftermath of Mohammad's death. It was during the early Abbasid period, a time of expansive growth for Muslim societies, that Islamic laws and jurisprudence (fiqh) began to take shape, transforming the image of Muslim women to be more in line with the civilized cultures of antiquity, drifting away from the early Muslim community of Medina.

In this study, we explore the intriguing question of how certain aspects of Islamic viewpoints and jurisprudence on women may have been influenced by Sasanian/Zoroastrian traditions. The Iranian culture and creeds played a unique and influential role in shaping the newborn Islamic civilization, particularly during the first half of the second century AH when the Islamic Empire was at its zenith, with Mesopotamia acting as its heartland.

Our investigation draws attention to the cultural continuity of Zoroastrian/Sasanian matrimonial customs and their incorporation into early Muslim jurisprudence. While Zoroastrianism and Islam may differ in their interpretations of marriage and wifehood's meaning and purpose, a significant number of Zoroastrian traditions found a place within Islamic Family Law, with exceptions for those clearly affirmed or prohibited by the Quran.

This scholarly work sheds light on the intricate historical interactions between Iranian culture and Islamic civilization, unveiling the nuanced influences that shaped the perception of women's roles and rights within early Islamic societies. By examining the parallels and departures from Zoroastrian traditions in Islamic jurisprudence, we gain valuable insights into the cultural and legal dynamics that shaped the status of women in the ancient Islamic world.

Acknowledgment

I would like to express my sincere gratitude to all those who have contributed to the completion of this book. First and foremost, I am deeply indebted to my supervisor, [Supervisor's Name], for their unwavering guidance, invaluable insights, and continuous support throughout the research and writing process.

I extend my heartfelt appreciation to my colleagues and friends who provided encouragement, constructive feedback, and stimulating discussions that enriched the content of this work.

I am also grateful to the institutions and libraries that granted me access to the resources necessary for conducting comprehensive research.

Finally, I would like to acknowledge my family for their patience, understanding, and unwavering belief in my abilities.

Without the contributions of all these individuals and institutions, this book would not have been possible.

Copyright Page

Early Islam and Zoroastrian Customs
Alvin R. Poole

Copyright © 2023 by Alvin R. Poole

TABLE OF CONTENTS

LIST OF FIGURES

NOTES ON TRANSLATION AND TRANSLITRATION

In this thesis, I translated the Persian and Arabic sources that have no English translations. In case of the Quran, I utilized the translation of the Quranic verses by Saheeh International, which I found more convincing. For translation of Zoroastrian sources in Old and Middle Persian I have relied on the English translations of the prominent scholars of the field except when I use the New Persian version of the text, for instance, *Mēnōg ī Xrad,* translated to New Persian by late professor Ahmad Taffzzoli. The transliteration system of the *International Journal of Middle East Studies* (IJMES) has been employed for some Persian and Arabic words.

LIST OF ABBREVIATIONS

Av.	Avestan
AWN	*ArdāWirāz-Nāmag*
BCE	Before the Common/Current Era
CE	Common/Current Era
CHI	Cambridge History of Iran
d.	Died
DD	*Dādestān ı Dēnıg*
Dk	*Dēnkard*
EI	Encyclopedia of Islam
EIr	Encyclopedia Iranica
GBd	*Great Bundahišn*
MHD	*Mādayān ī Hazār Dādestān*
MX	*Mēnōg ī Xrad*
PRDD	*Pahlavi Rivāyat accompanying the Dādestān ī Dēnıg*
PRA	*The Pahlavi Rivayat of Adur-Farnbag*
REA	*Rivāyat of Ēmed ī Ašawahištān*
Sns	*Šāyest-ne- šāyest*
Vd	*Vıdevdād*
AH	Lunar *Hejrī* calendar [After *Hejra*]
SH	Solar *Hejrī* calendar

CHAPTER 1

INTRODUCTION

Women and men originated in a single Self. They are two co-existing forms of a single reality--Quran 4:1.

I was merely a freshman at the University of Tehran School of Engineering when I decided to practice Islam. I had been raised in a secular family and knew very little about Islam, its branches, and its schools of thought. Influenced by the writings of Ali Shariati, I felt prepared to believe in a conscientious world with absolute beauty, rationality, justice and compassion at its core. Indeed, at that time, unlike today, Islam and its name were not under attack, on one side by the Islamic extremists – in almost every majority Muslim country – and on the other by those who take these extremists' actions for face value of Islam and criticize and condemn the religion accordingly. My journey in search of the possibility of a just and moral life for every human being has driven me to a deep study of Islam thus far. Through the years, and in spite of finding such a system of beliefs and practices in the Quran, as the most authentic and undisputable source of Islamic worldview, I have experienced and witnessed many unjust ideological claims and rules against Muslim women, both in Islamic jurisprudence and in the legal institutions of contemporary Muslim societies.

As Lapidus states, "there are myriad historical, geographical, socioeconomic, religious-doctrinal, and legal differences within the category of women in Islam,"[1] which makes religion just one of the numerous influential elements, including class and culture, in the life of Muslim woman. Nevertheless, and without denying the above fact, my observation as a Muslim woman and a researcher in Islamic Studies led me to the fact that there is a tremendous distance between

---

[1] Ira M. Lapidus, *Islamic Societies to the Nineteenth Century: A Global History* (Cambridge, England: Cambridge University Press, 2012), 181.

1

the teachings of the Quran and the knowledge that Muslim jurists utilize to make religious laws.

For instance, in the story of the origin of the creation of male and female in the Quran, there is no

evidence of Judeo-Christian narration of the Fall, the negative role of Eve, or the story of "the

rib." However, there are many *hadiths* in Muslim literature that confirm the biblical narration of

creation and have been used to confirm women's inferiority.[2] If so, then where did those rulings

and beliefs come from? My curiosity and studies found their way to the gradual construction of

Islamic jurisprudence in its historical context. Of course, many traditions in Muslim societies

originated from the ancient patriarchal cultures of Middle Eastern societies. Although male

scholars and jurists did add certain Quranic elements to their legislation, I share with Behnam

Sadeghi the belief that jurists utilized reason and religious sources to solely justify the existing

social order and prevailing culture. He writes, "what is thought to be the outcome of

jurisprudence, namely the laws, are actually the starting point for the jurist. The end product, on

the other hand, is an interpretation that reconciles the law with the textual sources."[3]

The authorities that have proclaimed "these rulings as Islamic," in fact, interpret the

Quran or the huge mass of egalitarian and spiritual Islamic texts in favor of male superiority,

which was an ancient, pre-Islamic prevailing cultural reality, partially inspired by non-Muslim

religious practices, beliefs, and cultures, among them Sasanian Zoroastrianism.

---

[2] Barlas writes, "None of the thirty or so passages which describe the creation of
humanity by God in a variety of ways is there any statement which could be interpreted as
asserting or suggesting that man was created prior to woman or that woman was created from
man. In fact there are some passages which could – from a purely grammatical/ linguistic point
of view – be interpreted as stating that the first creation was feminine, not masculine!" Asma
Barlas, *Believing Women In Islam: Unreading Patriarchal Interpretations of the
Qur'ān* (Austin, TX: University of Texas Press, 2011), 135.

[3] Behnam Sadeghi, *The Logic of Law Making in Islam: Women and Prayer in the Legal
Tradition* (New York: Cambridge University Press, 2015), xii.

Based on my hypothesis, I will argue that as the greatest political power and culture in the Iranian plateau and Mesopotamia, the Iranian/Zoroastrian customs and culture should have left their trace in the Islamic law and culture; and the most relevant to the life of the Muslim women is their trace in the Muslim family law. I will attempt to answer the following questions: Did Muslims develop family law based on their original text, the Quran? Is there any evidence to show a degree of acculturation of the Muslim Arabs who had settled in the previous territory of Sasanians in Mesopotamia? Considering some radical distinctions in their point of view on marriage and its ontological purposes, did Muslims emulate the teachings of Zoroastrianism to conceptualize the concept of an ideal Muslim woman? What is the resemblance and distinction between marriage and divorce law in those two traditions? Why did some traditions continue and others go extinct?

My research project explores the common elements in marriage and divorce laws of the two legal systems of the late Zoroastrian Sasanian Family Law and the early Muslim jurisprudence around seventh century CE in Mesopotamia. The chosen time and place is a matter of significance, given that the seventh century CE is an inflection point in the history of Mesopotamia, while the region as the heartland of Sasanian Empire has been conquered by Arab Muslim troops and became a prominent center of Islamic civilization as well as the birthplace of Muslim jurisprudence.

Muslims generally consider those rulings as the true understanding of God's will, embodied in the Islamic Sharia. However, the majority of the family laws contradict the Quranic verses, which considers man and woman of the same nature and equal in the eyes of God. The traditional strategy to solve such contradiction resorts to *hadith*, the alleged sayings of the prophet and his companions. By presenting those sayings as another source of law making, jurists practically neglected the Quranic solutions for constructing a new social order and replaced it with *hadith*, which almost match their traditional or existing social order. My objective is to illustrate that a major portion of the Muslim family law is similar to the Zoroastrian family law, and since those similarities have no legal trace in the Quran, they were, therefore, adopted from other sources than the Quran, such as (and highly likely) Zoroastrianism. This will raise questions about the validity of the Muslim jurists' claim regarding the sacred origin of the Islamic family law.

The answer to the question of where rulings that have regulated Muslim women's lives come from certainly has theoretical significance and practical consequences for them. Theoretically, by answering the questions and revealing their non-Quranic origins, Muslim women may practice liberation and equality as a pious Muslim with a clear religious conscience, since even thinking about equality and rejecting the gender inequality imposed by the Muslim jurists has been considered a sin. Practically, it may lead to the establishment of a new order in favor of not only Muslim women but also the appreciation of the religion itself amongst the contemporaries. Thus, in spite of the historical nature of this research, it serves as an urgent human rights matter in the lives of women across the countries where the Islamic family perspectives and traditions have been codified in their legal systems.

Methodology

My approach in examining marital laws and customs of those two traditions of Sasanian and early Muslim Iraq has been informed by my egalitarian, yet religious system of beliefs as well as feminist epistemology. I strongly believe there is a perfect confluence between Islamic ideology and feminism; while the Islamic worldview and numerous Quranic verses deny human inequality based on race, gender, or social status, feminism seeks repudiation of sexism and gender inequality.

The nature of my study requires analyzing historical documents and narratives, however I do this research from a feminist perspective; hence while epistemologically, I situate myself in my research as a Muslim woman, for whom both gender inequality and misinterpretation of profound egalitarian Quranic worldview is her concern. I mainly utilize those methods of textual analysis and historical criticism in order to conduct comparative studies of some legal and religious texts from two traditions while considering their historical context.

As a researcher in the field of women in religion, concerned with women's rights, an activist for gender equality in the Muslim tradition and Islamic countries' civil law, as well as a woman who has lived for decades under the Islamic law and is fully aware of the social and personal hardships that such law imposes on Muslim women, my research would examine all the research materials through the lens of feminist epistemology. The method for such interdisciplinary inquiry would be a blend of textual and historical analysis. Although those methods are traditional research methods, gathering and analyzing data from a feminist standpoint will affect both the methods and the results. I will examine both the primary sources and the works of contemporary scholars regarding the study of Sasanian Zoroastrianism and early Islamic traditions. Zoroastrian literature, same as Muslim literature, was written down mainly after ninth/fifteenth century[4] when papermaking prevailed in the Muslim lands. While most Zoroastrian texts were written after ninth/fifteenth century, a few were compiled before the Arab invasion of Iran. They are, however, reflective of numerous aspects of the Sasanians' laws

---

[4] Everywhere in this paper the phrase like: ninth/fifteenth century means ninth century based on Muslim calendar (AH) which is same date as fifteenth century Common Era (CE).

and customs. Islamic sources consist of primary history sources and secondary sources in which the early Islamic family law has been discussed. In addition to the primary sources, I enjoyed the works and opinions of prominent contemporary scholars of these fields.

I will utilize feminist standpoint theory to illustrate how Muslim and Zoroastrian male scholars' perspectives, which were shaped by their sociopolitical practices, even though, in spite of their ideological variance, produced a very similar family law, except for the cases that the Quran explicitly pardoned or forbade. My findings certainly will challenge Muslim jurists' traditional law-making process and their claims regarding the objectivity of their inferences derived from Islamic religious sources.

History of Scholarship

In regards to the Sasanian Zoroastrian primary sources related to family law, two books played a major role, *M□day□n □Haz□r D□dest□n* (MHD) or *The Book of A Thousand Judgments* and *Riv□yat of Emed□ıA□awahi□ı□n* (REA). While both contain materials related to women more than other Sasanian sources, the former, broadly believed, has been written briefly before the Arab conquest of Iran and the latter was dated at around three centuries later. I also utilized other Zoroastrian sources, mainly investigating Zoroastrian myths, morals and history, including, *D□nkard* (Dk), *D□dest□n ı □D□nıg* (Dd), the Pahlavi *Riv□yat of Adurfarnbag* (PRA), *M□n□g ı □ Xrad* (MK), and *Vıdēvd□d* (Vd). My secondary sources consist of books and articles by prominent scholars of Zoroastrianism who have written on Zoroastrian and Sasanian history, jurisprudence and particularly Zoroastrian family law. Below is a brief report of some major works on Zoroastrianism on women and family law.

Bartholomae's papers and speeches about women at the time of the Sasanian Empire is the first attempt to examine women's rights and roles under Sasanian/Zoroastrian legal system.

His translation of the newly discovered MHD, which is assumed to be the only existing "legal work on pre-Islamic Iranian jurisprudence which has survived from the Zoroastrian period,"[5] was the main source of his investigation. The book, which was compiled in the form of question/answer, is a combination of actual court and hypothetical cases,[6] many of which pertain to women's position in the Sasanian society. Additionally, I should name a salient Sorbonne University doctoral thesis, "Iranian Family Prior to Islamic Period" by Ali Akbar Mazaheri[7]; later, Mazaheri continued as a prominent scholar of Iranian Studies in France. Although that work was written in 1938, some of Mazaheri's suggestions regarding family relations in ancient Iran are still remarkable. For instance, the guardianship of a daughter who married without the permission of her father/guardian would not transfer to her husband; rather, it would be postponed until her son reaches puberty at which time the legal right of guardianship would be transferred to the son.[8] The following works related to women and family in Sasanian period have been published half a century later by scholars such as Mansour Shaki, Anahita Perikhanian, Maria Macuch, Bodil Hjerrild, Albert de Jong, and Jenny Rose.

In addition to his extensive research on various aspects of the ancient Iranian culture, Shaki greatly contributed to the study of the Zoroastrian Sasanian family law, including numerous articles as well as encyclopedia articles. Maria Macuch studied Sasanian family law in topics such as "Pahlavi Marriage Contract," "The Structure of Kinship in Sasanian," "Temporary

---

[5] Maria Macuch, *"M□day□n □Haz□r D□dest□n,"* in *Encyclopedia Iranica,* 2005, accessed October 15, 2016, http://www.iranicaonline.org/articles/madayan-i-hazar-dadestan.

[6] Ibid.

[7] Translated into Persian from French. Ali Akbar Mazaheri, *Khanevadeh Irani Dare Rozagar Peesh as Islam,* trans. Abdollah Tavakkol (Tehran: Ghatreh, 1994).

[8] Mazaheri, *Khanevadeh Irani,* 91.

Marriage," and "Incestuous Marriage." Another prominent work belongs to Bodil Hjerrild, who studied Zoroastrian family law in three Zoroastrian books that have been compiled in three different periods of their history, covering the period from the time that religion functioned as state religion to the time when they lived under Muslim conquerors.

After the Islamic revolution in Iran (1978 CE), a new trend of Iranian Studies in the West led to comprehensive research efforts regarding the study of Persianate world. A fantastic phenomenon of the 1980s in the field of Iranian Studies, *Encyclopedia Iranica*, was launched in 1982, based at Columbia University. The contributors defined their concern with the Iranian history, culture, languages and literatures, embracing the geographical regions of contemporary Iran and Afghanistan as well as parts of the Middle East, the Caucasus, Central Asia, and the Indian subcontinent.[9] So far, 1,300 authors and numerous articles on every aspect of the Iranians' lives, including topics concerning feminism, wifehood, and matrimonial issues have been published.

Islamic sources that have been incorporated into present work consist of primary and secondary works. I utilized the primary works, including *The History of □abari, Farsnama,* and *The Muqaddimah* by Ibn Khaldun, *The Best Divisions for Knowledge of the Regions* by Al-Maqd□s□,[10] Al-Masudi's *Mur□j* and *The History of Yaghubi* for historical background chapter as well as analytical part. In addition to the primary sources in Arabic and Persian, I enjoyed such works as "Divorce, Hadith-Scholar Style: From al-Darimi to al-Tirmidhi" by Scott C. Lucas and "Chapters in Marriage and Divorce: Responses of Ibn Hanbal and Ibn Rahwayh" by Susan A.

---

[9] See *Encyclopedia Iranica.*

[10] Also has been read Muqaddasi.

8

Spectorsky, in which the legal opinions and works of the leading Muslim jurists were translated from Arabic to English.

The topics regarding women in Islam have been vastly studied within the last few decades, either from a historical or legal perspective, many of which had a focus on women's rights in Islam and Muslim countries by scholars such as Nabia Abbott, Leila Ahmed, Amina Wadud, Asma Barlas, Ziba Mir-Hosseini, Fatima Mernissi, Riffat Hassan and the like. I will discuss their views throughout the next chapter, the "Historical Background."

Due to the comparative nature of this paper, I will further study the scholarly works on Islam/Zoroastrianism relations. Numerous research attempts have been made to illustrate the cultural continuity or adoption of beliefs and creeds from previous religions and cultures by the Islamic world during the process of transforming Islam from a simple faith to a complex religious institution.[11] In case of family law, however, the study of this continuity (Zoroastrianism to Islam) has rarely produced an informative work. The reason may be due to a lack of adequate comparative study on Zoroastrianism in the academic inquiries. In fact, the probability of continuity and adaption in family law and customs in a specific region is higher than that of other social institutions, considering the fact that, in case of social changes, family structure and law is the most conservative and enduring element of a human group.

Haleh Emrani and Fatemeh Sadeghi have conducted the most relevant study to the present study. Emrani carried out a scholarly comparative study of three religious traditions of Zoroastrianism, Judaism and Christianity within the Sasanian Empire for her doctoral thesis at University of California, Los Angeles. Iranian Women's Studies scholar and activist, Fatemeh

____

[11] See Yarshater and his sources. Ehsan Yarshater, "The Persian Presence in the Islamic World," in *The Persian Presence in the Islamic World* (Cambridge: Cambridge University Press, 1998), 4-13.

Sadegi's study[12] offers a remarkable research regarding sexuality in the ethical views of various Muslim and Zoroastrian schools of thoughts from three centuries before Islam to the fourth century of Islamic calendar. Sadeghi illustrates how the perspective of all these different schools and views on sexuality and womanhood in general are almost similar and based on the centrality of male sexual desires, manifested in the rigid division between male and female as well as a strong tendency to control female body and sexuality. Her research is the closest to the present research.

Chapters

In chapter 2, I will examine four different topics pertaining to the historical background of my research. First is a review of Sasanian Empire at the advent of Islam and a few decades later, the conquest of Iran by Muslim troops. It consists of a review of the structure of Sasanian society, including its class system, religious traditions, family order and moral codes, as well as the gradual changes on the legal position of women. Due to the geographical significance of Mesopotamia, I also review that region and its socio-political structure as well as its religious traditions in the late Sasanian period and early Islam. This is followed by a brief indication to the Iranians' gradual process of conversion to Islam. The next section attempts to illustrate the salient role of Persianate world on the construction of Islamic civilization and the influence of Iranian culture over the establishment of new religious institutions of Islam through quoting scholarly opinions and referencing academic sources. The third part is allocated to such topics as the configuration of family law in two traditions and the occurrence of some plausible adoptions. The final division skims the different opinions regarding the women's position in family and

---

[12] Fatemeh Sadeghi, *Jensiyat dar Ara e Akhlughi: as Gharn e Sevvom Pish as Islam tu Gharn e Chuhurrom e Hejri* (Tehran: Negahe Moaser, 1394 HS).

society in Arabia before and after Islam as well as in Mesopotamia through the end of the second century of Islamic calendar. It is worthy to note that by fulfilling the purposes of my paper, and considering the fact that traditions and customs always involve gradual changes, I will examine the late Sasanian and the early Muslim tradition around Mesopotamia.[13]

In chapters 3 and 4, I will go through the Zoroastrian and a variety of Muslim types of marriages and divorces and the resemblances and differences between them, trying to answer questions such as which traditions persisted after the Sasanians and which ones were not accepted by the Islamic traditions. For instance, next-of-kin marriage was not only absolutely prohibited by Muslims, but also, just after a few centuries of Islamic era, Zoroastrian communities denied the existence of such practice in their history. Furthermore, I will attempt to find an answer to the question: Since Muslims confirmed some of Zoroastrian traditions regarding marriage and divorce, why do the rest have no trace in the Islamic world?

After a survey regarding different types of dissolution of marriage in both traditions in chapter 4, I will discuss some unique aspects of Muslim traditions based on: the Quranic verses such as *Idda,* waiting period; the Quranic regulation regarding triple divorce; and some unique Quranic solutions against wife-harassment,[14] which according to the Quranic rules may lead to divorce. In addition, the financial arrangement between a husband, wife, and their families, both at the time of marriage or dissolution of marriage, has been compared and contrasted.

---

[13] I will discuss the process of formation of Muslim jurisprudence and the significance of Mesopotamia/Iraq in this process in chapter 2.

[14] This happens when husband either sexually abandons his wife as a means of punishment or accuses her of adultery without the Quranic required proof, which is testimony of four just witnesses who saw the intercourse with their own eyes.

CHAPTER 2

HISTORICAL BACKGROUND

Sasanian Empire

I. Background

The historical background of this paper will review the history of two remote territories

of the Arabian Peninsula and Persia along with the story of their encounter in Mesopotamia.

After the peaceful conquest of Babylonia by Cyrus the Great, the founder of Achaemenid

Empire, in 539 BC, Persia became "the first real world-empire of ancient history"[15] with the

slogan "into subjection every nation without exception."[16] Two centuries later, the Achaemenids

fell by the hands of the Hellenistic powers in 330 BCE. The Hellenistic state of Seleucid was

replaced by Parthian dynasty in 171 BCE. The Sasanians came to power over Iranian plateau by

defeating last Parthian king. Wiesehofer states,

> When on 28 April 224 [CE] the Parthian King Ardavan (Artabanus) IV laid down his life
> in the battle against his challenger Ardashir, this marked the beginning of the end of the
> almost 500-year-old Arsacid reign over Iran. The new masters from the "house" of Sasan,
> who had begun their ascent as local dynasts of Istakhr near Persepolis and extended their
> domain since 205/06 … in the following years came into possession of all the Parthian
> territories, as well as north-eastern Arabia.[17]

---

[15] Wilhelm Eilers, "Iran and Mesopotamia," in *The Cambridge History of Iran*, vol. 3.1,
Seleucid, Parthian and Sasanian Periods (Cambridge: Cambridge University Press, 2008), 481.

[16] See FIGURE 1.

[17] Josef Wiesehofer, *Ancient Persia: from 550 BC to 650 AD* (London, England: Tauris,
2011), 153.

The royal house of Sasan also served as the custodian of the Fire Temple of Anahid at Istakhr. They established the Sasanian Empire, "claiming that they were the inheritors of the ancient kings and destined to revive their glory and reunite all peoples of Persia."[18]

FIGURE 1. Achaemenid Empire, the first real world-empire of ancient history.[19]

The Sasanians were the last Persian dynasty before the Arab conquest of Iran. They ruled over a vast part of the Western Asia from 224-650 CE.[20] During the four centuries of their sovereignty, they became one of the two greatest powers in the ancient world, Persia and Byzantine Rome.

They founded a national state with a national religion and a civilization that was far more Iranian in character than that of the Parthians. They established a central power strong

---

[18] Shapur A. Shahbazi, "Sasanian Dynasty," in *Encyclopedia Iranica*, 2005, accessed October 15, 2016, http://www.iranicaonline.org/articles/sasanian-dynasty.

[19] "Achaemenid Empire" (map), Iran Chamber Society, accessed May 4, 2017, http://www.iranchamber.com/history/achaemenids/achaemenids.php.

[20] See FIGURE 2.

enough to curb the turbulent feudal aristocracy, built up a well-trained regular army, and provided the country with an efficient administration.[21]

Regarding the significance of the Empire, Christensen points to two characteristics of the Sasanian Empire: central administration and state religion[22] – their traditions remained for centuries after their decline,[23] as I discuss in the section on "The Persian Presence in the Islamic World." Nöldeke praises Sasanians as one of the excellent developments in the history of the orient; the royal house that could survive for 400 years and in the end brought to the throne a king like ☐osrow An☐irav☐n.[24] Muslims could not reach the economic status that the Sasanians enjoyed, even in their most glorious period of the Abbasid Empire.[25]

---

[21] Roman Ghirshman, *Iran: From the Earliest Times to the Islamic Conquest* (Middlesex, England: Penguin Books, 1978), 289.

[22] Christensen, *Ir☐n dar zam☐n-i S☐s☐n☐y☐n* (Tehran: Nigah, 2010), 49.

[23] Ibid., 166.

[24] Theodor Nöldeke, *Tarikh.i. Iranian va. Arab.ha dar Zamane.i. Sasanian* (Tehran: Anjoman Asar Melli, 1378 HS), 677.

[25] Ibid., 678.

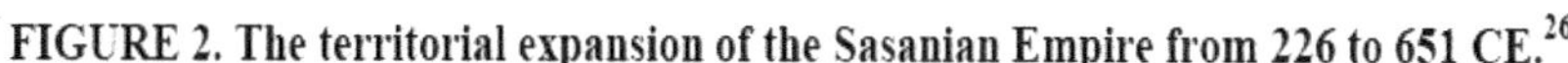

FIGURE 2. The territorial expansion of the Sasanian Empire from 226 to 651 CE.[26]

II. Sasanian Society

The Iran plateau embraced both settled populations and nomadic tribes, however,

Sasanians were urban-minded and had "urbanization plan" and "state-building program"; "it was

not an accident that by the end of Sasanian period their heartland, Mesopotamia, had the largest

population density in the pre-modern period."[27] Although the structure of the Iranian society had

been justified according to the Zoroastrian worldview, the economic and social forces were the

---

[26] Alonso Constenla Cervantes, "Territorial Expansion of the Sasanian Empire" (map), Ancient History Encyclopedia, May 17, 2013, accessed June 25, 2016, https://www.ancient.eu /image/1190/.

[27] Touraj Daryaee, *Sasanian Persia: The Rise and Fall of an Empire* (London: I. B. Tauris, 2008), 39-40.

real bases of their class divisions. The clergy, the military, farmers and artisans are the four

divisions in the Avestan concept of the social classes.[28] It is written in *Dinkard,*

> And those among the servants of the Mazdayasnian religion who are Athornans (priests)
> of the good religion ought to consider him as their ornament and luster. Those who tire
> Arthestars (warriors) ought to consider him as their warrior's armor. Those who are
> Vastariosh (husbandmen) ought to deem him as the sufficing happiness of their
> agriculture (husbandry). And those who are (of the) Hutokhsh (merchant and artisan
> class) ought to look upon him as the dress they wear.[29]

However, after the development of the Iranian society those divisions slightly changed to the

four groups of the clergy, the military, the scribes, and the artisans; the scribes including various

administrators, as well as physicians, poets, and astronomers; and the artisans, including

peasants, traders, cattle breeders, and those who earned their livings.[30]

From another perspective, the population of Iran could be divided into two groups: the

nobility and the masses – as Daryaee suggests.[31] In this regard, the nobility, with their lineage

claims, vast properties, and harems as well as multiple wives, were generally free of all

taxation.[32] Furthermore, the clergy, military leaders, scribes, and others in the immediate service

of the king represented a second level of the social hierarchy exempt from the poll tax.[33] On the

other hand, the majority of the population was required to pay taxes. They were restricted to one

---

[28] Mansour Shaki, "Class System iii. In the Parthian and Sasanian Periods," in *Encyclopedia Iranica,* 1992, accessed October 15, 2016.

[29] Darab Dastur Peshotan Sanjana, *Dinkard,* vol. 3: 179, Avesta, accessed October 13, 2015. http://www.heritageinstitute.com/zoroastrianism/outsidepages/avestaorg/dinkard.htm.

[30] Mujtaba Minuvi, trans. *Namah-'i Tansar bi-Gushnasp* (Tehran: Khvarizmi, 1975), 57.

[31] Daryaee, *Sasanian Persia,* 49.

[32] Christensen, *Ir□n dar Zam□n,* 98-105.

[33] Ibid., 362.

or, in rare cases, two wives and to ownership of a small piece of land; religious teachings encouraged them do to not save more than 300 *sters,* to not curse their rulers, and to not imitate the nobles.[34] The number of rules regarding the institution of slavery shows the high development of it in the Sasanian society; "By that time slaves had apparently become the chief producers in society."[35]

The Sasanian Empire was a crossroad of major trade routes between the Mediterranean world and East Africa on one side, and Central Asia, China and India on the other. Yet, trade was not limited to products, ideas were exchanged as well. The geographical location of the Sasanian Empire made it a meeting point of many ethnic and religious groups. It was a land of many populations who spoke a multitude of languages and following diverse beliefs. Also, it was heir to a civilization that had continuously existed over many thousands of years. This vast empire was home to countless communities of various religions living in relative peace. Although the Sasanian Empire had a state religion, the people of the Empire were mostly free in their religious practices. It is interesting that the Iranian plateau was the birthplace of Manichaeism,[36] the place that Babylonian Talmud had been collected, and where the Christian Church of the East emerged. "The Sasanian's imperial ideology relied on ethnic and religious pluralism, where the

---

[34] Mansour Shaki, "Citizenship ii. In the Sasanian Period," in *Encyclopedia Iranica,* 1991, accessed October 15, 2016, http://www.iranicaonline.org/articles/citizenship#pt2.

[35] Shaki, "Class System."

[36] "Dualistic religious movement founded in Persia in the 3rd century AD by Mani who was known as the "Apostle of Light" and supreme "Illuminator."" "Manichaeism," *BritannicaOnline,* 1998, accessed October 15, 2016, https://www.britannica.com/topic/Manichaeism.

leaders of the different religious communities managed their own internal affairs, while

representing their people in interaction with the royal administration."[37] Daryaee writes,

> By the fifth century CE, the state had realized the importance of the religious minorities
> and attempted to co-opt them into a system of governance where according to legal
> precepts, all would be considered simply as mard / zan [illegible]ahr "man/woman citizen (of the
> Empire)." Each community was bound by their local religious tradition and under the
> jurisdiction of their Rabbi and/or Priest. When there were cases, which were between
> people of different religious communities, the state court had precedence. Although
> Zoroastrian law was the basis of state law, the imperial system had created a system to
> co-opt all citizens of the empire.[38]

III. The Patriarchal Agnatic Family

The patriarchal agnatic family was at the core of the Zoroastrian/Sasanian social order,[39]

including the father as the head and guardian of family, mother as the principal wife, unmarried

daughters (married daughters belonged to their husbands' households,) and sons as well as other

members related through marriage, adoption and blood. Bondsmen and their families could also

be added. The members of this social unit "were bound by a highly developed set of legal

prescriptions and a strict moral code."[40] Only a mentally sound male member of the family who

has reached the age of fifteen could be the guardian of a family after his father. In the absence of

such a male successor and by the necessity of the existence of a protector of the wife, the child,

and the sacred fire in the house, a Zoroastrian believer should appoint a guardian for his family.

---

[37] Emrani, "Marriage Customs of the Religious Communities of the Late Sasanian
Empire: An Indicator of Cultural Sharing" (PhD diss., University of California, Los Angeles,
2011), 1-3, accessed October 15, 2016, http://proquest.umi.com/pqdweb?did= 2599379101&sid
=1&Fmt=2&clientId =1564&RQT=309&VName=PQD.

[38] Daryaee, *Sasanian Persia*, 56.

[39] Shaki, "Family Law i. in Zoroastrianism," in *Encyclopedia Iranica,* 1999, accessed
October 15, 2016, http://www.iranicaonline.org/articles/family-law.

[40] Ibid.

The father or guardian of the family had absolute control over his household. A father could sell his wife and children or give his children away to slavery.[41]

> The father was both guardian and owner of his children, who were obligated to obey him; in particular, a daughter was required to pay verbal obeisance to her father or guardian three times a day, standing before him with arms folded and vowing compliance with his wishes, requests, and demands. If a child failed in his filial duties or disobeyed the father three times, he was considered "punishable by death." The mother's role was simply to bear children, and she had no ownership rights.[42]

Still, there were certain obligations and unavoidable responsibilities for the head of the family and guardian. Broadly speaking, the head of a family or guardian was obliged to support his "patriarchal agnatic family" regardless whether he and his wife were in a principal marriage.[43] If a daughter or sister commits adultery or marry without the permission of her guardian while needing support, there was another thought that the guardian could not simply refuse to support her. There are some passages in the MHD talking about a man "who enters into sexual intercourse with a woman who has no definite guardian and if a child is born from this intercourse but the woman does not have sufficient property to support herself and the child, then this man must support the child until his majority and the woman until the child reaches his

---

[41] Anahit Perikhanian, *The Book of a Thousand Judgments* (Costa Mesa, CA: Mazda, 1997), 95.

[42] Mansour Shaki, "Children iii. Legal Rights of Children in the Sasanian Period," in *Encyclopedia Iranica,* 1991, accessed October 15, 2016, http://www.iranicaonline.org/articles/children-iii.

[43] Shaki, "Family Law."

majority."[44] In case of a violation of law by the subject, the head of the household is financially responsible, given he was aware of the violation.[45]

IV. Legal Position of Women

According to the old law, a woman had no legal rights. She was considered a thing rather than an individual, similar to a slave. She was in the full custody of the head of the family who could be her father, guardian or husband. Any earnings and gifts she receives would belong to the head of family.[46] She had a legal price of 500 *sters*, equal to the price of a regular slave.[47] However the price might be altered by the social status and wealth of a bride's father.[48]

Nevertheless, during the late Sasanian period and shortly before the Arab conquest of Iran, the social status of women gradually improved.[49] This process could be observed by the legal debates preserved in MHD.[50] Elman suggests, the process was motivated and/or accelerated by two factors: first, a shortage of adult upper-class males caused by the Black Plague, which began in the middle of the sixth century CE in Byzantium and Iran and lasted for the next two

---

[44] Perikhanian, MHD, 101.

[45] Ibid., 27, 95.

[46] Christian Bartholomae, *Zan dar □uq□q-i S□s□n□* (Tihr□n: □unbi□-i Mustaqill-i Zan□n-i □r□n dar □□ri□az Ki□war, 1982), 40.

[47] Mansour Shaki, "The Sassanian Matrimonial Relations." *Archiv Orientálni□* 39, (1971): 322- 45, accessed October 15, 2016, https://archive.org/details/TheSassanianMatrimonial Relations, 324.

[48] Daryaee, *Sasanian Persia*, 170.

[49] Bartholomae, *Zan dar Hoghough*, 40.

[50] As it mentioned before, the MHD compiled before Arab conquest of Iran, contains decisions from the late Sasanian period and earlier; thus it demonstrates the gradual change in the position of women in practice.

centuries; and secondly, the continuous wars of the sixth century CE. "In the end, an upper-class Iranian woman was permitted to manage the family estates, and thus represent the estate in court, give testimony, alienate her husband's property, inherit a double- share from her husband and a half-share from her father, and sometimes choose her own mate."[51] A daughter could not become an executor of the family estate as long as there was a son to fill this role; if there were no male offspring, however, then the oldest unmarried daughter was required to discharge her father's liabilities.[52] She also could be appointed as the guardian of the family fire only by her father's will.[53]

It is noteworthy that women of high rank such as the queen and the mother of the king had more autonomy in their activities and decision-making. They had their own seals and vast properties; they "engaged in hunting, drinking and feasting with men, and wore elaborate costumes."[54] The history of the Sasanian Empire shows the sovereignty of two queens, in spite of the negative standpoint of the Zoroastrian clergy and religious texts. Even though those two queens "were the only legitimate surviving members of the Sasanian family in the seventh century CE, the acceptance of their rule and the benevolent remembrance of them by the Sasanian sources suggest that they were accepted by the clergy as well."[55]

---

[51] Yaakov Elman, "Marriage and Marital Property in Rabbinic and Sasanian Law," in *Rabbinic Law in Its Roman and Near Eastern Context* (Tubingen: Verlag von J. C. B. Mohr (Paul Siebeck), 2003, 267-70.

[52] Perikhanian, MHD, 159.

[53] Ibid., 245.

[54] Daryaee, *Sasanian Persia*, 59.

[55] Ibid.

V. Mesopotamia and Arab Conquest of Iran

Another relevant area to this research is Mesopotamia, which was divided between Sasanian territory, two local dynasties, and a variety of tribal peoples. Morony expresses religious structure of Mesopotamia as "a segmented society composed of separate religious communities," including Persian Magians, Jews, and Christians (Nestorian & Monophysite).[56] Located on the far western borders of the Persian Empire, Iraq comprised of Arabs and Arameans more than Persian population, however, according to the Sasanian documents, it had been categorized as an Iranian part rather than the *"Aniran"* part of the empire. The name "Iraq" which is presumed an Arabic word, in fact, was derived from Middle Persian; it means lowlands;[57] Iraq had been a part of Iran since the Median period, more than a thousand years before the Arab conquest of Iran. Zoroastrians' distribution of population included the higher classes of society divided between the countryside, where they owned vast lands and the capital city, Ctesiphon, where they possessed houses and governmental positions such as "army officers, civil servants, judges, and feudal lords … The Jews were chiefly farmers, but to some extent also dwelling in cities, concentrated around Sura, Pumbadita, and above all Nehardea … The majority of the population were Arameans, speaking East Aramaic dialects, as did the Jews."[58] Due to their common religion with Romans, Christians were considered the most unreliable ethnic group of the region.

---

[56] Michael G. Morony, "Religious Communities in Late Sasanian and Early Muslim Iraq," *Journal of the Economic and Social History of the Orient* 17, no. 2 (1974): 113.

[57] Wilhelm Eilers, "Iran and Mesopotamia," in *The Cambridge History of Iran* vol. 3.1, *Seleucid, Parthian and Sasanian Periods* (Cambridge: Cambridge University Press, 2008), 481.

[58] Geo Widengren, "Āsōristān," in *Encyclopedia Iranica*, 1987, accessed October 15, 2016, http://www.iranicaonline.org/articles/asoristan.

FIGURE 3. Mesopotamia in the late Sasanian and the capital city of Ctesiphon.[59]

The Euphrates formed Iran's true western borders[60] beyond which the Sasanians' Arab

allies, the Lakhmid dynasty, resided. That small territory of Hira had been protecting the western

borders of Persia against the nomadic Arabs of the desert as well as against the Byzantines and

their allies in Syria. Shortly before the Arab conquest of Iran, the Persian king overthrew the

Lakhmid dynasty and replaced it with a Persian governor: "The fortunes of the Lakhmids and

Sasanians were so intertwined that within just over thirty years of the ending of Lakhmid

independence in 602 CE, Sasanian dominion over Iraq crumbled totally under Arabs from Najd,

impelled by the new faith of Islam."[61]

---

[59] "The Sasanian Xwārvarān or Quarter of the West, Which Included Mesopotamia with
the Capital City of Ctesiphon" (map), *Encyclopedia Iranica*. December 15, 2006, accessed June
25, 2016, http://www.iranicaonline.org/articles/iraq-i-late-sasanid-early-islamic.

[60] Eilers, "Iran and Mesopotamia," 483.

[61] Clifford Edmund Bosworth, "Iran and the Arabs Before Islam," in *The Cambridge
History of Iran*, vol. 3.1, *Seleucid, Parthian and Sasanian Periods* (Cambridge: Cambridge
University Press, 2008), 596.

After the domination of Muslims over the Arabian Peninsula and a few years after the

death of the prophet Muhammad, Arab troops marched toward Iraq and the Persian Empire's

western borders. Zarrinkub states, historical reports show there was no premeditated plan to

attack Iran. Fighting against the rebels in the peninsula and Yemen prepared the Muslim Army

and encouraged them to attack further lands. "Here almost without any obstruction they took

over a population of Aramaic cultivators ready to accept the Arabs as liberators."[62] The royal

power of the Sasanians was defeated very rapidly and Ctesiphon was occupied by Arab troops,

however the conquest of the entire Iranian land took a few decades. Zarrinkub's discussion on

the causes of this easy and unexpected victory of the Arabs was summarized by these sentences,

> The chief cause of the downfall of the Sasanians was the material and spiritual
> bankruptcy of the ruling class, which especially became apparent after the bad
> government of Khusrau Parviz, and which must account for the crumbling of so great a
> power before the attacks of a hungry people newly arrived on the scene; newly arrived,
> but inspired by the sense of walking in the way of a Lord whose message had been
> brought to them by their Prophet, and filled with ardor for adventure.[63]

This fast conquest of the main part of Persia may be related to the fact that the Arabs were

familiar with Persians, especially in Iraq where they had contacts.[64] Nevertheless, the abjection

of Persians did not last for a long time. Daryaee states,

> The conquest brought Asia closer together and now Arabs, Persians, Indians and the
> Chinese met each other on the Silk Road again, and with less strife. After Wahram's
> death the Persians had to wait only 40 years to topple the Arab rulers at Damascus, and
> by the ninth century, they would establish their own independent dynasties in Persia.
> Even then the Muslims rulers, be it Persian, Arab, or Turkish, remembered the Sasanians

---

[62] Abdolhussain Zarrinkub, "The Arab Conquest of Iran," in *The Cambridge History of Iran,* vol. 3.1, *Seleucid, Parthian and Sasanian Periods* (Cambridge: Cambridge University Press, 2008), 11-12.

[63] Ibid., 17.

[64] Rubin Levy, "Persia and the Arabs," in *The Legacy of Persia* (Oxford, England: Clarendon Press, 1989), 61.

and claimed to be the descendants of Sasan in one way or another. The family of Sasan was never forgotten.[65]

VI. Conversion

The Iranians' gradual process of conversion to the new faith lasted until the $4^{th}/10^{th}$ century.[66] Interestingly, the conversion happened more in the east than the western part of the empire, in Mesopotamia and Fars, which were conquered first. It happened in the Northeastern part of the Empire, Transoxiana, where the Arab troops reached while pursuing the last Sasanian king and later built their own settlements, with the early conversions happened in the vicinity of those Arab settlements. Fry writes, "By the ninth century [CE], except in areas of Fars province and pockets of non-Muslims elsewhere, the Islamic religion became everywhere predominant even in the countryside."[67] Certainly the relation between Zoroastrians and Muslims had its complications, altered between necessity and hatred. Zoroastrian religious authority confirmed trade with Muslims, however prohibited interreligious marriage, and developed their own system of purity to maintain distance from outsiders.[68] "Nevertheless, today Zoroastrian communities limited its population in two edge-of-the-desert cities of Yazd and Kerman in Iran and Parsi community of India."[69]

---

[65] Daryaee, *Sasanian Persia*, 38.

[66] Claude Cahen, "Tribes, Cities and Social Organization," in *The Cambridge History of Iran*, vol. 4 (Cambridge: Cambridge University Press, 1975), 263.

[67] Richard Nelson Frye, *The Cambridge History of Iran,* vol. 4, *The Period From the Arab Invasion to the Saljuqs* (Cambridge: Cambridge University Press, 1975), xii.

[68] Jamsheed K. Choksy, "Zoroastrians in Muslim Iran: Selected Problems of Coexistence and Interaction During the Early Medieval Period," *Iranian Studies* 20, no.1 (2007): 29.

[69] Ibid., 30.

It is He who has sent among the unlettered a Messenger from themselves reciting to them His verses and purifying them and teaching them the Book and wisdom - although they were before in clear error -And [to] others of them who have not yet joined them. And He is the Exalted in Might, the Wise.[70]

There are a number of *haradiths*, authentic in Sunni and Shi'a Islam, reporting when the prophet recited these verses to his companions, they asked him who was these people that had not joined them yet? And the prophet answered: "the people of Salman," who was his first Persian disciple. The prophet continued, "If faith were on the highest star then men among these people would reach it." The *hadith* was repeated in many *hadith* collections, including Sahih al-Bukhari,[71] Sahih al-Muslim.[72] The *hadith* demonstrated how Muslims felt about the contribution of the Iranians in the formation of *Umma*, Muslim united society.

In fact, the Persians had always been considered "the second oldest ethnic and cultural zone of the Islamic world"[73] after the Arabs. Nasr recounts the members of the Persianate world as contemporary Iran, the Kurds, Afghanistan, Tajikistan, and parts of Uzbekistan and Pakistan. Nasr states, "It was the Persians who, along with the Arabs, built classical Islamic civilization,

---

[70] Quran, 62: 2-3.

[71] Narrated By Abu Huraira : "While we were sitting with the Prophet Surat Al-Jumu'a was revealed to him, and when the Verse, "And He (Allah) has sent him (Muhammad) also to other (Muslims)...(Quran 62.3) was recited by the Prophet, I said, "Who are they, O Allah's Apostle?" The Prophet did not reply till I repeated my question thrice. At that time, Salman Al-Farisi was with us. So Allah's Apostle put his hand on Salman, saying, "If Faith were at (the place of) Ath-Thuraiya (pleiades, the highest star), even then (some men or man from these people (i.e. Salman's folk) would attain it." Sahih Bukhari Volume 6, Book 60, no. 420.

[72] Sahih Muslim, Book 31, Chapter 59, The Merits of the People of Persia, accessed July 07, 2017, http://www.iium.edu.my/deed/hadith/ muslim/031_smt.html.

[73] Seyyed Hossein Nasr, *Islam: Religion, History, and Civilization* (New York: Harper Collins, 2007), 19.

and Persia has always been one of the most important artistic and intellectual centers of the

Islamic world."[74] In his grand history book, Ibn-Khaldun asserts, in detail, how the Islamic

society needs a variety of skills, which Persians had possessed from the time of the Persian

Empire. Regarding the Persian contribution on the construction of Islam as an institution, he

writes,

> It is a remarkable fact that, with few exceptions, most Muslim scholars both in the
> religious and in the intellectual sciences have been Persians. When a scholar is of Arab
> origin, he is Persian in language and upbringing and has Persian teachers. This is so in
> spite of the fact that Islam is an Arabic religion, and its founder was an Arab.[75]

About the Persian participation in producing religious knowledge, he reports,

> Thus, the founders of grammar were Sibawayh and, after him, al-Farisi and az-Zajjaj. All
> of them were of Persian descent…they invented the rules of (grammar) and made it into a
> discipline for later generations to use… Most of the hadith scholars who preserved
> traditions for the Muslims also were Persians…all the scholars who worked in the science
> of the principals of jurisprudence were Persians, as is well known. The same applies to
> speculative theologians and to most Quran commentators. Only the Persians (Persians)
> engaged in the task of preserving knowledge and writing systematic scholarly works.
> Thus, the truth of the following statement by the Prophet becomes apparent: "If
> scholarship hung suspended at the highest parts of heaven, the Persians would (reach it
> and) take it."[76]

These scholars from Persia did indeed convey part of their old traditions to the new

establishment of the Islamic civilization. There are numerous historical reports that reflect the

influence of Iranian culture over the establishment of new religious institution of Islam.

Zarrinkub states,

---

[74] Ibid.

[75] Ibn Khaldūn, *The Muqaddimah: An Introduction to History*, trans. Franz Rosenthal, vol.3 (Princeton, NJ: Princeton University Press, 1974), 311, accessed October 15, 2017, https://asadullahali.files.wordpress.com/2012/10/ibn_khaldun-al_muqaddimah.pdf.

[76] Ibid., 313.

While Islam abolished the class society of Sasanian Iran, in some respects it conformed
to what were also ancient Iranian ideas, such as the belief in one God, Allah, and the
devil, Iblis, the angels, the Day of Judgment, the Bridge of Sirat, Heaven and Hell; and
even the five diurnal prayers were similar to ancient Iranian cult practices.[77]

Almost the entire administration model of the Sasanians were imitated by the Muslim

government in the eastern provinces, including tax-collection, court of law, intelligence/postal

service, the state official, police officers, scribes, and the structure of the royal court during the

Abbasid period. Furthermore, the Abbasids adopted numerous cultural aspects of the Iranians.[78]

The topic, The Persian presence in the Islamic world, may be the subject of numerous studies,

beyond the limitations of the present research.[79]

The Construction of Law

Sasanians had a central government and an official religion that suggests the existence of

administrative and legal institutions and federal law. However, what we understand from MHD

is that Sasanian jurisprudence, particularly family law, did not maintain comprehensive legal

norms but rather the opinions of some prominent jurists.[80] A gradual change in the position of

women also has been recorded in the Zoroastrian religious texts, which indicates the overall

improvement of their social status. Furthermore, there was a practical distance between their old

tradition of the religious leaders and actual civil law, which was based on the society's needs and

necessities. While the former came from old traditions of Iranian societies around the first

---

[77] Zarrinkub, "The Arab Conquest of Iran," 30.

[78] Levy, "Persia and the Arabs," 60-88.

[79] For an informative report regarding the contribution of Persians to the construction of
Islamic civilization, see Ehsan Yarshater, "The Persian Presence in the Islamic World," and its
sources.

[80] Emrani indicates MHD refers to a law-book, which did not survive, but may have
contained some sort of legal norms for all citizens of the Empire. Emrani, "Marriage Customs,"
50.

millennium BCE, the latter was based on the gradual change of their political, economical,

educational and social relations and realities.[81] Thus there were differences between theory and

action. The changes in Zoroastrian family law continued even after the decline of Sasanian

Empire; in a study of three Zoroastrian texts, regarding four legal institutions, written before and

after the Arab conquest of Iran, Hjerrild illustrates "while, in a certain measure, the spirit of the

law remained the same, the interpretation of the letter of the law seems to have changed to quite

a remarkable degree between the Sasanian and the post-Sasanian era."[82]

Muslims usually believe that God sent His laws for them through the Quran and the

tradition of the prophet, *Sunnah.* Thus, Muslim jurists assume they should discover God's law by

understanding these materials. However, traditional Islamic law is not a single uniform legal

code but a diverse and sometimes controversial corpus, since Muslim jurists' perspectives along

with the reality of Muslim societies are continuously changing. Historically, the Quran as a

"spiritual and legal guide" was the heart of the Islamic Law from the very beginning.

Furthermore, the sayings and deeds of the prophet and his disciples were considered what

Muslims should follow. Thus, almost immediately after the death of the prophet, the Muslim

tradition of oral narration of the words and actions of the prophet and his disciples emerged. The

emergence of Islamic law specialists happened later, around the end of the 1st century and the

---

[81] Shaki, "Hoghough dar Iran Bastan," *The Great Islamic Encyclopedia,* 1391 SH,
accessed October 25, 2014, https://www.cgie.org.ir/fa/article/25241/%D8%AD%D9% 82%D9
%88%D9%82%D8%8C-%D8%AD%D9%82%D9%88%D9%82-%D8%AF% D8% B1 -
%D8%A7%DB%8C%D8%B1%D8%A7%D9%86%D8%A8%D8%A7%D8%B3% D8
%AA%D8%A7%D9%86--%D9%85%D9%86%D8%B5%D9%88%D8%B1-%D8 %B4% DA%
A9%DB%8C.

[82] Bodil Hjerrild, *Studies in Zoroastrian Family Law: A Comparative Analysis*
(Copenhagen: Museum Tusculanum Press, 2003), 7.

early 2nd century of the Islamic calendar;[83] however, it was not until the middle of the 2nd century

of the Muslim calendar that the first *hadith* collections were recorded, following the prevalence

of papermaking throughout Muslim lands.[84] The Islamic schools of law were established after

the second half of the 2nd century AH.

The adoption of Sasanian culture by Muslims first took place in Iraq, the old territory of

Sasanians. That place played a crucial role in the process of making Islamic law. Ahmed states

that Islamic society that was established in Iraq articulated many of the Islamic laws, which are

still valid.[85] Perhaps, Schacht's great interest in the "Hellenistic world" and "Roman Byzantine"

as his own cultural origin of the Western Civilization has something to do with his argument

regarding the heavy influence of Roman law on Islamic law during its first stage of development,

yet, more recent scholars in the field have denied Schacht's theory.[86] However, Schacht further

indicated the salient position of Iraq in the formation of Islamic jurisprudence. He argued, "the

evidence available to us now shows that Muhammadan legal science started in Iraq around A.H.

100. The development of doctrine in Medina was invariably secondary to and dependent upon

---

[83] Wael B. Hallaq, *The Origins and Evolution of Islamic Law* (Cambridge: Cambridge University Press, 2011), 64.

[84] Floor, William, "Paper and Papermaking," in *Encyclopedia Iranica*, 2005, accessed October 15, 2016.

[85] Leila Ahmed, *Women and Gender in Islam: Historical Roots of a Modern Debate* (Philadelphia: University of Pennsylvania Press, 2011), 19.

[86] Jany Jonas, "The Four Sources of Law in Zoroastrian and Islamic Jurisprudence" *Islamic Law and Society* 12, no. 3 (2005): 292.

that in Iraq."[87] He also admitted that the possible influence of Sasanian law on Islamic

jurisprudence could not be proved simply because of insufficient academic knowledge about

Sasanian law.[88] Interesting, Schacht also states, "We know little about the Syrian school of law

in early Islam, but we do know that the Syrians were influenced by Iranian reasoning."[89] In fact,

he denies the chance of transmission of Roman culture from Syria to the Islamic world, thus he

had to search Iraq for "Hellenistic influence" and the "rabbinic tradition," as the possible ways of

this transmission. New academic findings confirm not only the impact of Sasanian culture and

religion on the Islamic tradition, but also its great influence on Talmudic tradition. For instance,

Elman asserts, "Middle Persian attitudes and doctrines made inroads in many areas of

Babylonian rabbinic culture, in law, in theology, and in general cultural attitudes."[90]

Finally, Al-Maqdīsi points to the strategic geographical location of Iraq as a reason for its

centrality on Islamic sciences. He argues that the reason why great scholars from the remote

places such as Egypt and Syria, as compared to Iraq and Hejaz, could not maintain their

influence over Islamic sciences is because those scholars did not reside in Iraq and Hejaz: "if

---

[87] Schacht, Joseph. "Foreign Elements in Ancient Islamic Law." *Journal of Comparative Legislation and International Law* 32, no. 3-4 (1950): 13, accessed October 15, 2016, http://ww w. jstor.org/stable/754369.

[88] Schacht, "Foreign Elements," 10; Jonas, "The Four Sources of Law," 292.

[89] Schacht, "Foreign Elements," 13.

[90] Yaakov Elman, "Rabbinic Literature and Middle Persian Texts," in *Encyclopedia Iranica*, 2010, accessed October 15, 2016, http://www.iranicaonline.org/articles/talmud-ii.

these men had been on the route of the pilgrims, people from the east and from the west would have disseminated their systems."[91]

Women Around Arabia and Mesopotamia, Shortly Before and After Islam

The origin of gender inequalities in the ancient world was generally associated with the establishment of state-cities and its consequences, including the emergence of ruling class, military activities and class division.[92] The development of class differences produced veiling and seclusion, as Keddie states, "veiling and seclusion developed in the pre-Islamic Near East and adjacent areas as markers for urban upper and middle-class women, showing that they did not have to work and keeping them from stranger."[93]

Nevertheless, "the subjection of women" did not take place entirely and all at once; for a long time after that there were records of women as state rulers, priestesses and social honorees. In her study of pre-Islamic Arabia, Abbott found several Arab queens, "some two dozen of these, in a period of over sixteen centuries."[94] She argues, "this is by no means a poor showing, since we are dealing with peoples and territories whose history, for great stretches of this long period, particularly from the Arab approach, is known to us only in spots."[95] And it was just a few centuries before the advent of Islam that we lost their salient traces in Arabia, but still there are

---

[91] Abū ʿAbd Allāh Muḥammad Al-Maqdisī, *The Best Divisions for Knowledge of the Regions* (Reading, England: Garnet, 2001), 132.

[92] Gerda Lerner, *The Creation of Patriarchy* (New York: Oxford University Press, 1995), 22, 212-16; Ahmed, *Women and Gender*, 11.

[93] Nikki R. Keddie, *Women in the Middle East: Past and Present* (Princeton, NJ: Princeton University Press, 2007), 204.

[94] Nabia Abbott, "Pre-Islamic Arab Queens," *The American Journal of Semitic Languages and Literatures* 58, no. 1 (1941): 22.

[95] Ibid.

records of famous women in the pre-Islamic Arab Poems as well as records of priestesses in

Islamic sources.[96]

During the centuries before Islam, Arabia had different family structure and marriage

patterns. Tribal order of a group of extended family from a common ancestor and their

"collaterals and clients" lived together. "Alongside the agnatic clan, various forms of

polyandrous marriage of one woman to several men with varying degrees of permanence and

responsibility for paternity, including temporary marriages, were also known in Arabia."[97]

On the position of Arab woman on the eve of Islam, or as Tucker puts it, "the meaning of the rise

of Islam for gender issues,"[98] there are four distinct arguments, even though all of these opinions

are based on the same textual materials/sources. First, traditional Muslim scholars believe in the

"revolutionary nature of the rise of Islam for women" that used to live during the "age of

Ignorance," meaning pre-Islamic Arabia. Under the commentary of the verse 19 of chapter 4 of

the Quran, Shi'a famous commentator of the Quran, Tabatabaee writes,

> The Arabs of the era of ignorance counted wives of a deceased person as part of his
> inheritance if the woman was not the heir's mother, as history and traditions have
> reported. The heirs took the widow as part of their share; one of them threw a cloth on
> her and she became his property. If he wished, he married her, inheriting the deceased's
> marriage - without giving her a fresh dowry. If he disliked marrying her, he held her in
> his custody; then if he was so pleased, he gave her in marriage to someone and used her

---

[96] Nabia Abbott, "Women and the State on the Eve of Islam," *The American Journal of Semitic Languages and Literatures* 58, no. 3 (1941): 259.

[97] Lapidus, *Islamic Societies, 183.*

[98] Judith Tucker, "Gender and Islamic History," in *Islamic & European Expansion: The Forging of a Global Order* (Philadelphia: Temple University Press, 1993), http://www. iranicaonline.org/articles/family-law, 42-45.

dowry himself; and if he wished, he kept her in straitened condition, not allowing her to marry, until she died and he inherited her property, if she had any."[99]

Secondly, some took an exactly opposite standpoint, asserting that Islamic rulings and teachings limited women on many aspects of their lives; Leila Ahmed, Fatima Mernissi, and Nabia Abbott are amongst them. For instance, Ahmed considers Khadijah and Hind as pre-Islamic figures and Aisha as an Islamic one. Khadijah enjoyed her own trade, her marriage without a guardian, and with a man who was fifteen years her junior, as well as a monogamous and self-initiated marriage; Aisha, on the other hand, was restricted by veiling and faced a polygamous marriage.[100] But Ahmed failed to address Aisha as a leader in the battle of Camel who provoked people who were unhappy about the assassination of the third caliph and mobilized an army. Abbott and Ahmed further missed the point that after Hind was divorced, she borrowed money from the second caliph and enjoyed her own trade. The incident could have been considered a sign that Mohammad and his successors did not prevent women from having their own trade activities. The history of Tabari, under the events of year 23, narrated the story, "Hind bt. Utbah paid her respects to Umar ibn al-Khatab and asked him for a loan from the treasury of 4,000 [*dirhams*] with which to engage in business, and at the same time making herself responsible for (the sum). (Umar) lent her money and she took it off to the territory of Kalb, where she bought and sold."[101]

---

[99] Tabatabai, Muhammad Hussein, "Tafsir Al-Mizan - Allamah Muhammad Hussein Tabatabai," *Almizan*, accessed May 16, 2017, http://www.almizan.org/index.php, under the commentary of Quran 8:75.

[100] Leila Ahmed, "Women and the Advent of Islam." *Signs* 1, no. 4 (1986): 665-66.

[101] Mu☐ammad Ibn-☐ar☐☐ Tabari, *The History of Al-☐abar☐ (Ta☐r☐kh Al-rusul Wa☐l-mul☐k),* vol. 14 (Tehran, Iran: Asatir, 1996), 133.

A third group "minimizes the impact of Islam on the prevailing gender system."[102] For

instance, Nashat considers the gender egalitarian perspective in the Quran and the fair status of

women during the lifetime of the prophet, as a result of the prevailing traditions of the pre-

Islamic culture of Arabia.[103] On the other hand, Muslim scholarly activities began when Muslim

tribal communities of Medina transformed into an Islamic Empire, embracing the entire territory

of Sasanian Empire and part of Byzantine's lands. Thus, the Islamic jurisprudence was shaped

"under the influence of long-standing gender patterns of Mesopotamian heritage,"[104] considering

Islam as "merely an accelerant that precipitated the process of urbanization of Arabian

culture."[105]

Twenty-four years after Tucker's article, we can identify a fourth approach, which

implies that historically the rise of Islam led to the establishment of several women's rights

during the lifetime of the prophet Muhammad, even though the impact of those rulings soon

declined following his death. Eventually, during the first half of the second century AH or the

early Abbasid period when Muslim societies were expanding to become the largest empire of the

time, the majority of the Islamic law or *Sharia* developed and increasingly turned the image of a

Muslim woman into one similar to that of the civilized cultures around Mesopotamia and Middle

---

[102] Tucker, "Gender and Islamic History," 44.

[103] Guity Nashat, "Women in the Middle East, 8000 BCE to 1700 CE," in *A Companion to Gender History* (Oxford: Blackwell, 2006), 234.

[104] Tucker, "Gender and Islamic History," 44.

[105] Nashat, "Women in the Middle East," 229.

East; Amina Wadud,[106] Asma Barlas,[107] and Kecia Ali,[108] are among those scholars who support

this latter perspective. However, answering the question, to what extent the original teachings of

Islam had to do with these gradual changes? These scholars offer differing opinions.

While I accept the fourth approach, I believe that Nashat's argument above is fair and

reflective of pre-Islamic Arabian women's status with the exception of her assertion of a mere

transitory role of Islam; I would argue that the economic independency that the teachings of the

prophet brought about women[109] are far beyond a transfer of Mesopotamian culture, even though

the social force of patriarchy and Muslim male jurists did their best to meet the norms of the

prevailing local culture.[110] Nashat convincingly draws a picture of pre-Islamic Arabian women's

situation; she writes,

> Women in pre-Islamic Arabia lacked a secure position in what was a patriarchal society.
> A tribe required fewer women than men to protect it and bring in resources from raids or
> trade with other groups; consequently, surplus infant girls would be left to die. To
> compensate for the shortage of women, some Arabian tribes practiced polyandry.
> However, in pre-Islamic Mecca, where wealth from trade was increasing, a woman from
> a respectable family married only one man, whereas her husband could marry as many

---

[106] See Amina Wadud, *Qur'an and Woman: Rereading the Sacred Text From a Woman's Perspective* (New York: Oxford University Press, 2006).

[107] See Barlas, *Believing Women in Islam*.

[108] See Kecia Ali, "A Beautiful Example: The Prophet Mu□ammad as a Model for Muslim Husbands," *Islamic Studies* 43, no. 2 (2004): 273-291.

[109] Being the sole recipient of her dower, income and inheritance from parents, husband, siblings and children whom she survived, as well as the legal entity before God and state that she gained throw the Islamic orders.

[110] Many researches regarding Muslim women and Sharia court illustrate how Muslim women had access to juridical system before modern period; they could stipulate contracts, initiate divorce, or sue in court. See Mathieu Tillier, "Women before the Q□□□under the Abbasids" *Islamic Law and Society* 16, no. 3-4 (2009), and its footnotes; also see Amira el-Azhary Sonbol, *Women, the Family, and Divorce Laws in Islamic History* (Syracuse, NY: Syracuse University Press, 1996), chap. 4 and 5.

wives as he wished. When a woman married, her father or male guardian received the full bride price. Women who were divorced received no compensation, and they did not inherit from the husband. Some women did well if they married rich and generous husbands, but most women were left at the mercy of the male members of their family and tribes on their husband death.[111]

In case of divorce, "pre-Islamic Arab practices indicate that men generally had unrestricted rights to divorce, although they had to announce it publicly."[112] In the matrilineal marriages, the wife could easily divorce her husband, since her financial affairs were in the hands of her tribe. *Kitab al-Aghani* reports: "The women in the *Jahilia* [Pre-Islamic Arabia], or some of them, divorced men, and their [manner of] divorce was that if they lived in a tent they turned it around, so that if the door had faced east it now faced west ... and when the man saw this he knew that she had divorced him and did not go to her."[113] On the contrary, in a patrilineal union, when the marriage was a result of capture or purchase, the wife had no right of divorce. If the marriage was by a contract between the husband and the wife's tribe, though, even though she had no right to dissolution of the contract, "she could seek protection with her own people if ill-treated by her husband."[114] Also pre-Islamic divorce was not generally followed by the waiting period for women before a remarriage.[115]

Lapidus believes the value system that the prophet presented reflected many elements of pre-Islamic Arabian culture, but also significantly modified its context... "The moral and

---

[111] Nashat, "Women in the Middle East," 233.

[112] Labidus, *Islamic Societies,* 20.

[113] Ahmed, *Women and the Advent of Islam*, 669; Fatima Mernissi, *Beyond the Veil Male-Female Dynamics in Modern Muslim Society* (London: Al Saqi Books, 1985), 75.

[114] Jane I. Smith, "Women, Religion, and Social Change in Early Islam," in *Women, Religion, and Social Change* (Albany: State University of New York Press, 1985), 21-22.

[115] Ahmed, *Women and the Advent of Islam*, 669.

spiritual reform advocated in Quranic verses enhanced the status of women." It happened by identifying women, spiritually, equal to men and by recognizing their property rights.[116] Furthermore, prophetic practice hints at women's right to initiate divorce.[117] How did the prophet treat women? He writes,

> *Hadith* report him as regularly conversing with his wives and generally treating them with respect, patience, and gentleness... Little research systematically examines the Prophet's interactions with women who were not related to him as wives, daughters, or other relatives. From what we now know, he appears not to have imposed seclusion or avoided contact with women. When he first began preaching in Mecca, the sources report him teaching men and women together. They specifically depict the Prophet as making social visits to various female companions; many women other than his wives transmitted *hadith* from him. Women were present as political representatives at the Aqaba meeting between the Prophet and members of the Medinan community; later, women fought in raids and battles. Women are also reported to have provided food and nursed the wounded during battles.[118]

Nevertheless, after the prophet, Muslim women experienced a gradual decline of their freedom and rights; it happened during the next three centuries when Muslims became increasingly more in touch with the dominant cultures of Iran, Mesopotamia and Syria and later in Egypt and Spain. During this period, *hadith* collections and Quranic commentaries were produced and utilized as sources to articulate Islamic jurisprudence.

The Arab conquests of the Middle East and the construction of an empire out of a nomadic culture prompted conquerors to imitate the old Middle Eastern social and administrative patterns. Those sociopolitical changes affected the position of women in Islam, particularly those

---

[116] Lapidus, *Islamic Societies,* 183-84.

[117] Ibid., 183.

[118] Ibid., 184-85.

connected to upper class circles.[119] The minimal rights of slave women along with their charm

and easy accessibility degraded the free woman's rights and position, respectively in

jurisprudence and society.[120] Seclusion, segregation and veiling were the consequences of these

changes in Muslim women's lives.[121] There are historical reports that illustrate decline of free

women's status and advantages beside the comfortable life of slave girls in the courts and the

aristocrats' houses encouraged free but poor women to go to the slave market and offer

themselves for sale.[122]

During the Abbasid period, women had already been eliminated from social spheres,

except for some royal queens who had influence over their husbands.[123] It took nearly one

hundred years after the beginning of the Abbasids until the caliphs stopped marrying free women

who could challenge their husbands. The gradual decline of position of the upper class women

can be traced through the lives of the Abbasid queens. The first Abbasid queen, Umm Salama,

the only wife of Abu al-Abbas, the future Saffah, the first caliph of Abbasids, had already

married twice before sending Abu al-Abbas a marriage proposal.[124] At that time, he was a

handsome, young but poor man while rich Umm Salama "had outlived two distinguished

---

[119] Lapidus, *Muslim Societies,* 185.

[120] Kecia Ali, *Marriage and Slavery in Early Islam* (Cambridge: Harvard University Press, 2010), 6-8; Ahmed, *Women and Gender,* 67.

[121] Ahmed, *Women and Gender*, 80; Lapidus, *Muslim Societies,* 185.

[122] Hasan Ibrahim Hassan, *Tarikh al-Islam al-Siyasi wa-al-Dini wa-al-Thaqafi wa-al-Ijtima'i,* vol. 2 (Cairo, Egypt: Maktabaht an. Nehdhat al-Mesriya, 1974), 353.

[123] Ibid.

[124] Abu al-Ḥasan Alī ibn al-Ḥusayn ibn Alī Al-Masʿūdī, *Muruj adh-Dhahab wa Ma'adin al-Jawhar* (Tehran: Bungāh-i Tarjameh va Nashr-i Kitāb, 1965), 265-68.

Umayyad husbands … he promised her, on oath, never to marry another woman or even to take a concubine."[125] When the young man became caliph, he kept his promise despite incessant encouragement by the people in his court to break up his marriage. A rather funny story narrates how Umm Salama disciplined a man who dared to advise Saffah to take another bedfellow.[126] Saffah died in his early thirties and never had a chance to marry again. The next caliph, Mansur, also had a powerful wife who had married him before his reign. She demanded a written promissory that her husband "would take neither wife nor concubine for as long as she lived."[127] Umm Musa remained the only wife of Mansur until her death, even though later as a caliph, Mansur repeatedly tried to find a legal way to dismiss the agreement.

> Umm Musa always knew when a judge was being approached for that purpose, and her bribes never failed to reach the magistrate in question. In the end she named the chief justice of Egypt as the only judge to whom she would submit her case. He was, therefore, brought from his distant province to Iraq to try the case between the royal couple. Umm Musa produced her marriage contract as evidence, and the just judge decided the case in her favor.[128]

Ten years after he attained sovereignty, Mansur was informed of the death of Umm Musa in Hulwan; Tabari writes, "that night he was given a hundred virgins."[129]

Even though the next two caliphs, al-Mahdi and al-Harun, had four wives and many concubines, they still had powerful queens, Khaizuran and Zubaidah, respectively, who had

---

[125] Nabia Abbott, *Two Queens of Baghdad: Mother and Wife of H□r□n al Rash□d* (Chicago: University of Chicago Press, 1991), 11.

[126] Al-Mas□□d□, *Muruj*, 267-68.

[127] Mu□ammad Ibn-□ar□ Tabari, *The History of Al-□abar□* vol. 29 (Albany, NY: State University of New York Press, 1990), 127-128.

[128] Abbott, *Two Queens*, 15-16.

[129] Tabari, *The History,* vol. 29, 128.

influence over the king, the court, and the society. Abbott writes, "Khaizuran and then Zubaidah emerged from the privacy of the royal harem to the center of the stage of early Abbasid history. Each queen revealed, in turn, a vivid and colorful personality, the first determined to rule the state, the second eager to dazzle court and society."[130]

After the death of Mansur, Mahdi manumitted his slave girl Khaizuran, who already had two sons by him, and married her. She became the mother of two future caliphs, Hadi and Harun. "She was a former slave of Yemeni origin. She became very powerful because of her influence with Mahdi. Her position declined in Hadi's reign, but she regained much of her influence upon the accession of Harun."[131] Although, the historical sources speak of Harun's two hundred slave girls, amongst which were two dozens concubines who bore him several children,[132] he still had a prominent and powerful wife, his cousin, Zubaidah whose major political interest centered around the heirship of her son, Mohammed al-Amin. There are numerous stories regarding her endeavors to secure her son's succession. However, after the assassination of Amin by Ma'amon's army she did nothing but wear black, mourn, and write a soft and sad letter to Ma'amon in which she addressed him as the caliph.[133]

---

[130] Abbott, *Two Queens*, v.

[131] Tabari, *The History,* vol. 29, 177.

[132] Abbott, *Two Queens*, 138.

[133] Ibid., 160-61.

By the end of the Golden Age,[134] almost a hundred years after the beginning of the

Abbasids, the caliphs stopped marrying free women who could challenge their husbands.

Lapidus writes, "under the early Abbasids, royal women had their own households; but after the

death of Harun, caliphs did not marry, and their mothers were the chief women at court. By the

tenth century, women were housed in a special structure within the royal palace."[135]

---

[134] Due to its prosperity in politics, economics, and culture, the middle of the eighth to about the middle of the ninth century CE has been named as The Golden Age of the Abbasid Empire.

[135] Lapidus, *Muslim Societies,* 185-86.

CHAPTER 3

MARRIAGE IN TWO TRADITIONS

Sasanian/Zoroastrian Marriage

The family structure and relations of Zoroastrian Sasanians can be explained by

understanding some of their principal notions and beliefs. First, in the early Sasanian period,

family was an independent social unit, economically, militarily and judicially. However, over

time the authority of the head of family was partially transmitted to the state and jurists while the

authority of the father over his family remained intact.[136] Furthermore, the legal rights of a

family unit went to that collective unit, represented by the father/guardian, rather than to the

individuals; as a result, women, children and slaves were left with almost no legal rights.[137]

Lastly, the main purpose of matrimony, as has been defined in Zoroastrian sources, was to

produce an heir, the male one who would protect the household and maintain the religious rituals

after the death of his father/guardian. The necessity of providing a male successor pushed

Sasanian/Zoroastrian law to invent a unique way to maintain an heir for a man who was not

biologically able to produce one. It was this concern that precipitated a variety of types of

Zoroastrian marriage.[138] In addition, it should be added that what I will discuss here is related to

the free, commoner matrimony rulings and customs rather than that of the privileged social class,

since "citizenship was closely bound up with the individual's social class, sex, and religious and

---

[136] Mazaheri, *Khanevadeh Irani,* 15.

[137] Bartholomae, *Zan dar Hoghugh,* 31.

[138] Maria Macuch, "Zoroastrian Principal and the Structure of Kinship in Sasanian Iran," in *Religious Themes and Texts of Pre-Islamic Iran and Central Asia: Studies in Honour of Professor Gherardo Gnoli on the Occasion of His 65th Birthday on 6th December 2002* (Weisbaden: Reichert, 2003), 231.

ethnic affiliation …Whereas women of noble birth could rise even to the highest office of the state, lower-caste women were traditionally regarded in law as a kind of property."[139]

I. Principal Marriage

The principal marriage occurred between a man and a virgin woman who was from the same social status. In this kind of marriage, the permission of the bride's father or guardian, the consent of the bride, and a marriage contract were required. Furthermore, the amount of the money that the husband should pay to the bride's family must be mentioned in the contract; legally, women were seen as equal to children and slaves, and the average money that the husband should have pay was about 2000 *drahms,* equal to the price of a slave.[140] These features may have been altered based on the social rank of the couple's families.

The bride was the principal wife and she had the full rights the law allowed for a wife while the wives from other types of marriage did not have her privileges.[141] The husband and the wife were the heir of one another in this world and each other's spouse in the other world.[142] The principal marriage should be with a family of the same social status. Fathers could not give their daughter away without their consent. On the other hand, a girl could not refuse marriage past the age of fifteen. It was necessary for her father to marry her off as soon as she reached puberty.[143]

---

[139] Shaki, "Citizenship."

[140] Shaki, "The Sasanian Matrimonial Relations," 324.

[141] Daryaee, *Sasanian Persia,* 60.

[142] Katayoun Mazdapour, "Barresi Chand Estelah Farsi Miyani," *Zaban Shenakht* (2010): 14.

[143] Daryaee, *Sasanian Persia,* 352-54.

Guardianship. The concept of guardianship has been discussed in chapter two, yet given the almost absolute authority that the husband had over his family, some further points can be added. The husband could sell his wife;[144] he had authority to give his wife[145] or his daughter[146] to a proxy marriage, without their consent, if he did not have a son. The dower, or the marriage portion bride received from her husband, belonged to her paterfamilias. The property she brought to her husband's family, even though it formally belonged to her, she had no access to those, since she had no legal position before state.

The duty of a wife before her husband was absolute obedience. A husband could give his wife to another marriage without her consent.[147] In exchange, the principal wife was entitled to maintenance, shelter and inheritance. The rights and responsibilities of the head of family have been elaborated and sometimes altered by time or judicial opinions.

Age of marriage. During the Sasanian period, the age of marriage for boys was fifteen, which is generally the age of puberty for boys in that region. For girls, in geographical locations such as in the Iranian plateau, puberty occurred between the ages of nine and twelve. In the Sasanian tradition, a girl might marry after nine but no later than twelve.[148] From the Sasanian legal perspective at the time, it was considered a great sin if a girl refused to get married or her

---

[144] Perikhanian, MHD, 95.

[145] Ibid., 33, 131.

[146] Ibid., 103.

[147] Ibid., 229.

[148] Daryaee, *Sasanian Persia*, 60.

guardians failed to marry her away by the age of fifteen.[149] The aforementioned age range is the age of consummation for a marriage, however, practically, a minor child could marry off even earlier.

Ideal wife. The ideal wife had three salient characteristics: beauty, benignity, and obedience. In the book of *Mēnōg ī Xrad* [MX], the question of who is superior over all women in her rank was answered by these characteristics—young (lovely), beautiful, devoted, good-tempered, and modest.[150] Another passage states: a wife must obey and worship her husband,[151] given that the marriage was solely focused on the needs and the will of the husband. A woman with whom her husband could not live in happiness was considered the worst wife.[152] Furthermore, the disobedience of a wife could even jeopardize her children's right to inherit from their father.[153]

Social rank. Due to the social hierarchy of Sasanian society, Iranians were required to marry within their social class. According to the Pahlavi Texts of *Andarz-i-poryotkaesan*, if a prince desires to marry a shepherd's daughter or a wealthy man from a lower class would want to marry a girl from a family of pure blood—a noble family—it would in time lead to chaos and social disaster.[154]

---

[149] Shaki, "Family Law."

[150] Ahmad Taffazzoli, trans. *Mēnōg ī Xrad* (Tehran, Iran: Tus Publishers, 1364 HS), 78-79.

[151] Ibid., 56.

[152] Ibid., 49.

[153] Shaki, "Family Law"; Perikhanian, MHD, 253-59.

[154] Mazaheri, *Khanevadeh Irani*, 47.

Marriage contract. Mazaheri states, during the Sasanian period, Iranian marriage had

for several centuries relied on a contract, whereas "buying the bride" and even "stealing the

bride," was and still is in practice among some other neighboring nations.[155] In Iran, the practice

had been abrogated by the teachings of Zoroaster.[156] In the Sasanian period, marriage was by

definition an arranged matrimony that had been established by a contract between the

family/guardians of the bride and the groom. Both Macuch, in her article "The Pahlavi Model

Marriage Contracts in the Light of Sasanian Family Law," and Ilya Yakubovich, in his article

"Marriage Contract in Pre-Islamic Period," examined a template marriage contract from Thirteen

century CE, used by Zoroastrian officials, preserved in the Codex MK. The codex could

resemble a pre-Islamic Sasanian marriage contract, since the structure of the contract is in

agreement with the juridical norms of the late Sasanian "Book of the Thousand Judgments" and

the post-Sasanian Pahlavi Rivayats.[157] According to the Codex, the main features of a

regular/principal marriage included the following elements: the guardianship of the wife is

transferred from her agnate family to the husband's family; she becomes the "mistress of the

house"; she and her children are the legal heirs of the husband who has responsibility for their

---

[155] For instance see, Kleinbach R, and Salimjanova L. "Kyz Ala Kachuu and Adat: Non Consensual Bride Kidnapping and Tradition in Kyrgyzstan," *Etnograficeskoe Obozrenie* 3, no. 3 (2011): 133-56.

[156] Mazaheri, *Khanevadeh Irani,* 33.

[157] Macuch, "The Pahlavi Model Marriage Contracts in the Light of Sasanian Family Law," in *Iranian Languages and Texts from Iran and Turan* (Wiesbaden: Harrassowitz Verlag, 2007), 184.

livelihood. Also, the contract maintains the wife's obligation to enter a proxy marriage in order

to provide her husband an heir, in case the husband proves to be barren.[158] Macuch writes,

> The bridegroom accepted the bride from the bride's father in this manner that the bride
> also should accept the following: As long as I live, I shall not deviate from the marriage
> with the bridegroom and his intermediary succession, and submissiveness, and obedience
> towards him, as well as from being an Iranian and practicing the Good Religion. And the
> bridegroom also accepted the following: As long as I live, I shall hold her dearly in
> marriage, established as mistress of the house, provided with food and clad with clothing,
> according to my status of husband and guardian and fitting the requirements of the times,
> well respected, and I shall regard the children born by her as my own original children.[159]

It was a religious obligation that a marriage should be concluded by the consent of the

bride. However, not only was marrying off a minor child without her consent widely practiced,

but also even after puberty the bride could not annul the contract. "If a girl of nine years has

attained to puberty, she cannot give herself in marriage to a man without the consent of a lawful

guardian, and turn away from the wifehood of that man; if she turns away, she is a sinner

deserving death, after a full year expires thereafter."[160]

Macuch's speculation regarding some passages of the Codex MK suggests that the

practice of giving the dower to the bride, instead of her father, was known in the Sasanian period.

The argument does not sound convincing. She argues,

> Our text not only explicitly states that the bride should give her consent to the proposed
> amount of money, but also names her as the sole recipient of the dower. We may
> conclude from the meticulously exact use of legal terminology that the original model of

---

[158] Ilya Yakubovich, "Marriage i. the Marriage Contract in the Pre-Islamic Period," in *Encyclopedia Iranica*, 2005, accessed October 15, 2016, http://www.iranicaonline.org/ articles/marriage-contract-in-the-pre-islamic-period.

[159] Macuch, "The Pahlavi Model Marriage Contracts."

[160] Behramgore Tahmuras Anklesaria, trans., *The Pahlavi Rivayat of Adur-Farnbag,* Avesta -- Zoroastrian Archives, 1938, accessed October 15, 2016, http://www.av esta.org/mp/ adurfarn.html.

our marriage contract dates from the Sasanian period and that the practice of bestowing the dower on the wife was already known in pre-Islamic Iran.[161]

As it was previously mentioned, due to the specific circumstances, around the end of Sasanian Empire, a principal wife in absence of her husband had some limited authority over family affairs. Some passages from MHD illustrates the mistress of the house may get involved in judicial activities;[162] however, she could not appeal to the court without a male guardian,[163] and she was not allowed to attend court even though "her consent was necessary."[164] The law book considers a principal wife unable to attend court or set up an appeal by herself. How, then, is a wife, especially a young bride, entitled to a dower, which means financial independency, and at least legal authority, over that dower? Macuch's argument is not convincing since the so-called dower is not bestowed on the bride. However, since the contract talks about what she can use from her husband's income after marriage, it seems like a kind of promise or regulation about her maintenance or, perhaps it is an imitation of the post-Sasanian Muslim dower,[165] based on Islamic regulation, where women had property rights.

Macuch translates the term *ahlawdad* as "pious, righteous gift" and *pad* as "purpose;"[166] thus, both Macuch and Yakubovich translated the term *"pad ahlawdad"* as "in accomplishment

---

[161] Macuch, "The Pahlavi Model Marriage Contracts," 200.

[162] Perikhanian, MHD, 53, 55.

[163] Ibid., 57, 59.

[164] Emrani, "Marriage Customs," 125.

[165] This kind of setting is not the original Muslim setting of paying dower, which was to pay dower in the beginning of marriage. Rather it is the jurists' later arrangement that brought relief for husbands by postponing the payments of dower.

[166] Macuch, "The Pahlavi Model Marriage Contracts," 195-96.

of a pious act." Although there is common agreement about this meaning of *ahlawdad* among scholars, Mazaheri's understanding of *pad ahlawdad* is totally distinct. He believes *pad ahlawdad* refers to the "righteous gift" that the bridegroom or his family pays to the bride's father, same as bride price.[167] Even though Mazaheri believes that the tradition was just, as E.B. Tylor put into words, "survivals"[168] of the ancient tradition of buying brides that had nothing to do with Zoroastrian tradition.[169] I suggest that paying dower to the bride was not a norm in the Sasanian period. Even today in Iran, after more than a millennium of Islamic traditions, the old Sasanian tradition, side by side with the Islamic one, has been practiced. Among Iranian marriage customs, the trace of 'bride price' could be observed. On the one hand, according to the Islamic tradition, the husband grants his wife a dower and the bride inherits her agnate family after marriage. On the other hand, according to the pre-Islamic tradition of Iran, the bride's parents send her to the husband's home with a dowry,[170] usually including home appliances,

---

[167] Mazaheri, *Khanevadeh Irani,* 73.

[168] "Survivals," in anthropology has been defined as "cultural phenomena that outlive the set of conditions under which they developed." "Survivals," *Britannica online,*

[169] Mazaheri, *Khanevadeh Irani,* 74.

[170] Price in her study of Iranian marriage ceremony writes, "A very important part of the pre-wedding activities is dowry preparation by the bride's family. Till very recently the girls were expected to prepare many of the items themselves. They were required to weave fabrics, prepare cloths and many in the poor families would weave carpets and rugs long before there was any talk of marriage. The tradition is very ancient. Herodotus mentions that Achaemenian Queen, Amestris, Xerxes's future wife made a magnificent outfit for the king with fabrics that she had woven and prepared before her marriage. Today dowry preparation is still practiced by almost all families. The bride's family will buy household items for the dowry. The higher the social status the more elaborate will be the dowry and it could include properties as well. The very modern professional couples with means do not follow this tradition. On the whole this is still very important and is practiced by the majority." Massoume Price, "Iranian Marriage Ceremony, Its History & Symbolism." Iranian Chamber Society, 2001, accessed October 15, 2016, http://www.iranchamber.com/ culture/articles/ iranian_marriage_ceremony.php.

furniture, cookware, and everything the couple need in their home.[171] Also, in many areas and among more traditional/poor families, the husband's family pays the wife's family. Today, there is no such term as "bride price" rather a more respectful term, "milk price."[172] The money is paid as a way to help the wife's family in preparing the dowry, especially among poor families. The tradition is more prevalent in Afghanistan, which is a part of the Persianate world, because of the lack of financial means.[173] It would be an evolved form of the old tradition of "bride price,"[174] since there is no such practice among Muslim Arabs.

Polygamy. Although middle and lower class men practiced monogamy and bigamy, wealthy men could practice polygamy depending on their wealth and social rank.[175] Nevertheless, Polygamy, except in some specific situations, was not considered a righteous act, even though the elite men had many concubines. It is written in Denkard, "As far as possible,

---

[171] Price, "Iranian Marriage Ceremony."

[172] The tradition continued under the name of *"Sheer Baha,"* in Persian means *"milk price,"* which the bridegroom's family pays to the bride's family before the bride transfers to her husband's household.

[173] See Valentine M. Moghadam, "Reforms, Revolutions, and 'the Woman Question,'" in *Modernizing Women: Gender and Social Change in the Middle East* (Boulder: Lynne Rienner Publishers, 2013), 85.

[174] Moghadam believes the practice is an abuse of Muslim *Mahr,* marriage portion; her suggestion did not consider the historical background of the practice; I believe *Sheer-baha* is the ancient practice of bride price that still survived in the poor areas, in Iran and other Persianate societies. See Valentine M. Moghadam, *Gender and National Identity: Women and Politics in Muslim Societies* (London: Zed Books, 1994), 85.

[175] Shaki, "The Sasanian Matrimonial Relations," 338.

(unless through necessity), a woman should not wed a second husband, nor a man a second wife, because such act, (according to the religion), is not a meritorious one."[176]

II. Consensus Marriage: Marriage Without a Guardian

A daughter who married without the consent of her guardian may face punishments such as losing her right to inheritance, at least partial or all financial support of her father/guardian, and the chance to become a principal wife in her marriage. However, according to some jurists, in the case where a mature girl would like to marry by her own choice yet the father cannot or does not give her in marriage, she could legally marry per her own permission, despite the fact that this kind of behavior was socially and culturally unacceptable.[177] In such cases the guardianship of the daughter did not transfer to her husband; rather, when her later-born son reaches the age of puberty he would become her legal guardian. In fact, the guardianship of the daughter remained in her father's house; its transmission was hindered until her son came to the age.[178]

III. Marriage by Proxy or Substitution

The necessity of the existence of a male heir created some sophisticated law and arrangements in the marital tradition. Elaborating by jurists, these kinds of marriages had different forms in different situations. According to an old belief, the spirit of a dead man who had no heir could not be saved in the afterlife: "When a man dies without a male heir, his wife or daughter should be given in marriage to one of his close relative in order to give birth to a son

---

[176] Sanjana, DK, vol. 5, Chap.18: On Women.

[177] Perikhanian, MHD, 75, 95; Nezhat Safa-Isfehani, *Rivayat-i Hemit-i Asawahistan: A Study in Zoroastrian Law: Edition, Transcription, and Translation* (Cambridge: Harvard University Press, 1980), 43.

[178] Mazdapour, "Barresi.e. Chand Esteluh," 15; Mazaheri, *Khanevadeh Irani,* 91.

who would be the legal heir of the dead man."[179] It was said that if anyone neglected this custom and duty, he was responsible for the death of numerous souls.[180] A man who has not a male heir should establish a proxy. The duty could be performed in different ways. First he can choose a man as a proxy son; second, if he has a young and productive wife, he can give her in a proxy marriage to usually—but not necessarily—a male relative. It was one of the cases that the husband was allowed to give his wife to a marriage, even without her consent, since she belonged to him in this and the next life. The children, begotten by his wife from the second marriage, belonged to him and among them, the first-born male was the successor. If he did not do so in his life, after his death a daughter, young widow, or a sister of his should enter a proxy marriage, likely to a close relative. In this case this female relative of the deceased was an "intermediary successor" or *ay□g□n*.[181] The child from this marriage then belonged to the deceased's family as a male heir.

Sometimes, however, there were no female relatives who could handle the duty. As a result, the patriarchs and the elders would establish *stur'ih*, substitution marriage, employing a man or a woman, to produce at least a son as the heir of the deceased man while the expenses were paid from the assets of the deceased man.[182] Regarding the difference between these institutions, Hjerrild states,

---

[179] Shaki, "Family Law."

[180] Ibid.

[181] Maria Macuch, "Inheritance: Sasanian Period," in *Encyclopedia Iranica,* 2004, accessed October 15, 2016, http://www.iranicaonline.org/articles/inheritance-i.

[182] Bodil Hjerrild, "The Institution of Sturih in the Pahlavi Rivayat of Aturfaranbag," in *Iranica Selecta: Studies in Honor of Professor Wojciech Skalmowski on the Occasion of His*

The difference between a čakar – or *ayokin* – marriage and the *stur'ih* is that the *stur* (the person providing the heir) might be either a man or a woman. Furthermore the *stur* did not necessarily belong to the close family circle, and, more importantly, a fixed amount of money/property had to be tied up in a trust, which the *stur* could not transfer to his/her own personal possession.[183]

In proxy and substituted marriage, there was no financial connection between the couple. The wife did not hold the same position as the principal wife, and her son was not the successor of his biological father but rather the heir to the deceased man.[184]

IV. Next-of-Kin Marriage

The most controversial type of marriage is next-of-kin marriage, marriage with close relatives, like a father, mother and siblings of the opposite sex. Historical evidences confirm the practice began among royal dynasties, was continued by commoners, and is tied to Zoroastrianism in the Sasanian period. While contemporary Zoroastrians deny the existence of such type of wedlock, "the description of incestuous bonds, its merits and advantages, is so precise in Pahlavi literature that it is impossible to ignore the evidence pointing to a society that not only allowed incest, but even encouraged it in all three forms[185] as the best possible alliance between the sexes.[186] There is a general academic agreement that the custom had survived at least until the ninth or the tenth century CE, three or even more centuries after the Arab conquest

---

Seventieth Birthday, edited by Wojciech Skalmowski and Alois Van Tongerloo, (Turnhout, Belgium: Brepols, 2003), 93.

[183] Ibid.

[184] Shaki, "The Sasanian Matrimonial Relations," 325-30.

[185] These forms include, mother and son, father and daughter, and brother and sister.

[186] Maria Macuch, "Incestuous Marriage in the Context of Sasanian Family Law," in *Ancient and Middle Iranian Studies: Proceedings of the 6th European Conference of Iranian Studies*, (Wiesbaden: Harrassowitz, 2011), 133.

of Iran. Daryaee states "anyone who can read Avestan or Middle Persian, along with the

attestation of the foreign sources can have no doubt whatsoever that this type of marriage was

practiced in Sasanian Persia."[187]

About the origin of the practice, next-of-kin marriage may be traced back to the early

Achaemenids, since according to Herodotus Cambyses was the first king to marry his sister.[188]

The custom has been observed onward until a few centuries after the Arab invasion of Iran and

in places like Iran plateau, Asia Minor, and Mesopotamia as well as Egypt.[189] Initiated by

Cambyses the Persian conqueror of Egypt, Gray points Egyptian dynasties and the desire to

"keep the royal blood absolutely pure" as the possible origin of the practice in Persia.[190]

However, considering the matriarchal nature of next-of-kin marriage and the close connection

between Elam and Iran, Frye implies that Elam, originally matriarchal, could be the source of the

practice.[191] On the other hand, denying the possibility of such "deep and abiding influence of

Elamites on Zoroastrian community," Boyce points out to the "early and struggling stage" of

Zoroastrianism when they had to practice incest, to preserve their small community and faith

from outsiders. She believes this hypothesis at least can explain why priests considered the act

---

[187] Daryaee, *Sasanian Persia*, 130.

[188] Louis Herbert Gray, "Marriage. Iranian. 2: Next of Kin Marriage," in Encyclopedia of Religion and Ethics Indexes, edited by James Hastings, vol. 8, 457, London: T&T Clark, 1915, accessed December 19, 2016, https://archive.org/details/in.ernet.dli.2015.56058.

[189] For a full account of the subject in the Zoroastrian and non-Zoroastrian sources, see Prods Oktor Skjærvø, "Marriage ii. Next-of -Kin Marriage In Zoroastrianism," in *Encyclopedia Iranica,* 2013, accessed January 30, 2015, http://www.iranicaonline.org/articles / marriage-next-of-kin.

[190] Gray, "Marriage. Iranian. 2: Next of Kin Marriage," 457.

[191] Frye, "Zoroastrian Incest," 449.

meritorious. Furthermore, she notes the fact that the term has an Avestan origin makes it originally from the East and an early stage of Zoroastrianism.[192] While an objection from Zoroaster himself was recorded in *Dinkard*, Gray poses the possibility of an even older origin, from Indo-Europeans or "the older Iranism."[193] Shahbazi puts "the blame" on the Magi and their influence on the Achaemenid royal court after Cyrus and by the time of Cambyses.[194]

Macuch connects the institution of next-of-kin marriage in its Sasanian context to the field of substitute succession. Referring to the structure of kinship in the Sasanian system and "the complete lack of an incest taboo,"[195] she suggests a "far more important fictive" role for the practice. She writes,

> It is… one of the most important prerequisites of Sasanian family law, allowing not only real marriages inside the nuclear family, but also far more important fictive consanguineous bonds which are unique and not to be found anywhere, except in a society that not only accepted incest on an ideological basis, but integrated it into its kinship system.[196]

But what caused the custom to be that prolonged? Menasce highlights the economic reason related to the Sasanian family structure and traditions, which made the family pay the dowry (inheritance) of their daughter to the husband's family at the time of marriage. Given the desire to keep the family's heritage and wealth intact, the aristocrats and upper class families preferred to have their daughters married with close relatives. Furthermore, astonished by the persistence

---

[192] Mary Boyce, *A History of Zoroastrianism,* vol. 2 (Leiden: Brill, 1996), 76.

[193] Gray, "Marriage. Iranian. 2: Next of Kin Marriage," 476.

[194] Shahbazi, A. Shapur. *Kooroush.e. Kabir (Cyrus the Great)*, (Shiraz, Iran: Mosavi Publisher, 1349 SH), 410-13.

[195] Macuch, "Zoroastrian Principal," 234.

[196] Ibid.

of the custom within the Mazdaean community, he believes the necessity of saving the

Zoroastrian faith while surrounded by Muslim communities would be another reason for next-of-

kin marriage after the conquest of Iran.[197] Daryaee points to the two periods of Sasanian history

in which the practice was intensified,

> I believe that advocacy for such a type of marriage was intensified in particular periods in
> Iranian history, namely the third century, when the Manichaeans challenged
> Zoroastrianism; and more importantly in the 6th century when Christianity became a
> major threat; and finally in the eighth and the ninth centuries when state support for
> Zoroastrianism had collapsed and the Muslims were gaining numbers and becoming the
> new elite.[198]

Topic is still under debate.

Another question is if the Muslim communities of Iran and Iraq knew about such

traditions that were intensely against their codes of conduct? There are many indications of this

type of Zoroastrian marriage in Islamic sources, jurisprudence and literature. Altering the

mythical root of the custom, Taalebi writes, the marriage is legal because Adam let his children

marry one another.[199] Masudi in *Moruj*, Tabari in his history, and many others reported the

existence of such a tradition among Zoroastrians,[200] which indicates they knew about the

tradition. In Jurisprudence, for instance, Muslim scholars discuss the inheritance of such people

who are/were in next-of-kin marriages or were born to such union. In the preface of the Persian

translation of the Bartholomae's article, "Woman in Sasanian Period," Naṣīr ad-Dīn Ṭālib az-

---

[197] Jean Pierre de. Menasce, "Zoroastrian Literature After the Muslim Conquest," in *The Cambridge History of Iran,* vol.4, *The Period From the Arab Invasion to the Saljuqs* (Cambridge: Cambridge University Press, 1975), 552.

[198] Daryaee, "Marriage, Property and Conversion," 91.

[199] Skjaervo, "Next-of-Kin Marriage."

[200] Ibid.

Zam□ni, the translator, reports a narration from Jafar-i Sadig, sixth Imam of Shi'a, hearing one of his disciples addressing a Zoroastrian as a bastard, regarding the practice of next-of-kin marriage. The Imam blames him and abandons him, stating the practice is legal through their religion and thus honorable, and they should not be considered bastards or whoresons.[201] Rash□d Y□sami in his translation of Christensen's book also mentioned the story.[202]

About the length of persistence of the custom after the Arab invasion, the first objection was recorded during the eighth century CE. According to several authors, in Khorasan, a Northeastern province of Iran, around the eighth century CE, a Mazdean priest, prohibited the performance of the practice in the Mazdean community. As a result, he was accused of heresy and killed by the hands of Abu Muslim, the Muslim leader of Khorasan army through the conspiracy of Zoroastrian Priests.[203] Still there is evidence of performing next of kin marriage at the end of the 10th century CE. Saheb ibn Ebbad, grand *Vazir* of Buyid dynasty, mocked the incestuous marriage of Zoroastrians in a sarcastic poem, as □□ib az-Zam□ni, indicates.[204] Later they denied the existence of this kind of marriage. Yet to this day there are still some debates about it. Nevertheless, the custom survived in the form of marriage between cousins, which even in current day Iran is still recommended.

---

[201] Bartholomae, *Zan dar Hoghugh*, 20.

[202] Christensen, *Iran dar Zaman.e. Sasanian*, 436.

[203] Golam-Hosayn Yusofi, "Behafarid," in *Encyclopedia Iranica*, 1989, accessed October 15, 2016, http://www.iranicaonline.org/articles/behafarid-zoroastrian-heresiarch-and-self-styled-prophet-killed-131-748-49.

[204] Bartholomae, *Zan dar Hoghugh*, 19.

V. Temporary Marriage

Although there are no specific legal terms for temporary marriage in the Pahlavi legal texts, all forms of marriage could be contracted on a temporary basis.[205] In the Sasanian/Zoroastrian tradition the main reason for marriage was to produce children, chiefly a son. This son should maintain the continuity of the lineage by bearing the responsibility and duties of the late father. Therefore, in some circumstances, producing a successor was conducted by performing a marriage temporarily.[206] For instance, a proxy marriage could be temporary and terminated after providing a male heir.[207] A daughter, a wife, or a sister of a man without issue was obliged to enter into a proxy marriage to produce a male successor, a regulation that could happen on a temporary basis. According to the book of MHD, a principal wife may bear the obligation of becoming the *ay□g□n*[208] of her late husband for ten years in case her husband dies childless.[209] Another passage states that even if the husband is alive, he may give his principal wife away to another marriage to produce an heir for himself.[210] MHD 101, 4-8, shows the husband is able to give his wife, as a gift, to a co-religious bachelor who is in need of a wife,

---

[205] Maria Macuch, "The Function of Temporary Marriage in the Context of Sasanian Family Law," in *The Fifth Conference of the Societas Iranologica Europaea. Proc. of Ancient and Middle Iranian Studies (Ravenna, October 6-11, 2003)* (Milan: Edizioni Mimesis, 2006), 594.

[206] Ibid.

[207] Perikhanian, MHD, 131, 221.

[208] Some scholars believe the term *□akar* denotes to the deceased 's wife if she enters into a proxy marriage. The term turns to *ay□g□n* when the sister or daughter bears the task. See next page.

[209] Perikhanian, MHD, 203.

[210] Ibid.

producing for him an heir. Even though there is no particular text and verses that mentions the temporal identity of those two latter cases, Macuch assumes those marriages could also be temporarily contracted.[211]

On the other hand, even a principal marriage might be contracted for a limited period. MHD 23, 1-4 implies that if a man has a daughter but not a son he may give her daughter away to a principal marriage for a limited time of ten years. At the end of the period, the daughter enters a proxy marriage, as an *ayōgēn*, producing a successor for her father. Macuch believes "temporary marriage in Zoroastrianism was one of the most important means of using the fertility of a female to the fullest degree without having to give up the patrilineal line of descent."[212]

VI. Auxiliary Marriage, *čakarīh*

Representing some specific characters of Zoroastrian family law, *čakarīh* is a middle-Persian legal term describing an institution in which a woman marries a man while she does not have the full right of a principal wife such as the right of maintenance, inheritance, and guardianship. Her children did not have any claim regarding their biological father. In this account, both husband and wife would have been considered a *čakar*. The true meaning of the term is a matter of controversy. Bartholomae explains *čakar* as a wife who does not enjoy the full right of principal wife.[213] Shaki believes *čakar* is a term denoting a widow who has entered a levirate marriage at the death of her authorized husband in order to provide him with male

---

[211] Macuch, "The Function of Temporary Marriage," 592.

[212] Ibid.

[213] Bartholomae, *Zan dar Hoghugh*, 52.

offspring.[214] Macuch describes čakarīh as auxiliary marriage in which the bride remained in the lineage of her father or principal husband.[215]

Mazdapour explains the term with its social and financial properties based on Sasanian family structure and law. She believes čakarīh is an umbrella category for any wedlock that does not transfer guardianship of the wife and there is no financial connection, the right of inheritance, and maintenance, contrary to the principal marriage, between spouses.[216] The situation of a čakar wife has been defined in *Rivāyat of Ēmēd ī Ašawahištān* [REA] answer 7, 11-12,

> If a woman is a čakar, she is already helpless because of her being a čakar. Therefore it should not be repeated to her face, for she is sufficiently defenseless. Unless there has been especial promise or deal between them, a čakar wife, when her husband passes away, has no right to claim the property, nor food or provision from what her husband has left.[217]

The latter definition of čakarīh not only embraces other definitions but also includes marriage of a man to a widow, a woman without dowry, or union with a slave, as well as a woman whose husband gave her to another marriage as a gift. About the usage of the word čakar, Safa-Isfehani in her English translation of REA states:

> It would be appropriate to point that the word čakar, which is frequently used in this section, covers a wide range of meanings in Pahlavi texts such as: stepmother or father, or son or daughter, collateral wife, a widow or widower, a girl who has no brother or father when she marries. Even a father who has children other than those by his main

---

[214] Mansour Shaki, "Cakar," in *Encyclopedia Iranica,* 1990, accessed October 15, 2016, http://www.iranicaonline.org/articles/cakar-a-middle-persian-legal-term-denoting-a- widow-who-at-the-death-of-her-authorized-padixsayiha-q.

[215] Macuch, "The Function of Temporary marriage," 587.

[216] Mazdapour, "Barresi.e. Chand Esteluh," 17.

[217] Safa-Isfehani, REA, 53.

wife would be a □akar father. In short, it seems that most family relationships, which are not original and are somehow substituted, fall in the category of □akar.[218]

VII. Concubinage

In addition to those marriages, concubinage was practiced in the Sasanian Empire much like the other parts of the ancient world. While the ordinary people practiced monogamy, polygamy prevailed amongst aristocrats and the members of the courts. Common in society and culture, wealthy men and aristocrats had access to female sexuality with no restrictions, as is evident from the size of royal harems and the house of the privileged men. Ardashir I, the founder of Sasanian Empire, not only married his own daughter but also had three hundred and sixty "beauteous concubines."[219] The last powerful Sasanian king, Khosrow II, who was famous for being always in search of beautiful girls by his agents from all around the Empire, had twelve thousand women in his harem; three thousand of them were his concubines.[220] Reporting the battle between Crassus and Parthians, Greek historian, Plutarch, writes about Surena, second man of the kingdom and the leader of the Persian army. Even though he traveled in private, he had two hundred chariots for his concubines who also traveled with him.[221]

VIII. Mixed Marriage

Before the Arab invasion of Iran, mixed marriage with the member of other religious communities was solely allowed for men. There are some evidences that indicate mixed marriage

---

[218] Ibid., 160.

[219] Plutarch, *The Book of Ardashir*, The Internet Classical Archive, accessed October 15, 2016, http://classics.mit.edu/Plutarch/artaxerx.html.

[220] Mu□ammad Ibn-□ar□ Tabari, *The History of Al-□abari,* vol. 2 *(Ta□r□kh Al-rusul Wa□l-mul□k),* trans. Abu-al-Ghasem Puyandeh (Tehran, Iran: Asatir, 1996), 766.

[221] Plutarch, *The Book of Crassus*, The Internet Classical Archive, accessed October 15, 2016, http://classics.mit.edu/Plutarch/crassus.html.

had been practiced In the Sasanian period, even though legal documents regarding the regulation of such union do not exist.[222] For instance a passage in MHD 44.6-8 suggests the possibility of interfaith marriage. It states, "A man who has no wife, or one wife who is not Mazdean …".[223] In addition, Sasanian history recorded some famous Jewish and Christian queens.[224] Ibn Balkhi in the *Farsnama* states, Iranians used to marry women from all over the world but they do not marry off their daughters with anyone except their relatives.[225]

Islamic Marriage

Family law has always occupied a central place within the Islamic law; "together with inheritance law it is the only field of Muslim law that has remained nearly intact to the present day."[226] Multiple marriages are permitted to men, who could have up to four wives at one time.[227] However, with some interpretation of the specific verses of the Quran, Muslim jurists added unlimited concubinage for a man in Sunni and Shi'a jurisprudence as well as unlimited temporary marriages for men in Shi'a's. In Arabic, *Nikah* means sexual intercourse and defines any legal sexual activity in Islam between a man and a woman. There are two types of sexual relationship in Sunni jurisprudence: regular marriage and the purchasing of a slave woman. On

---

[222] Emrani, "Marriage Customs," 219.

[223] Perikhanian, MHD, 119.

[224] Emrani, "Marriage Customs," 220.

[225] Ibn Balkhi, *Farsnama*, ed. Guy Le Strange and Reynold Nicholson (Tehran: Asatir, 2005), 97-98.

[226] Jeanette Wakin, "Family Law ii in Islam," in *Encyclopedia Iranica*, 1999, accessed October 15, 2016, http://www.iranicaonline.org/articles/family-law.

[227] Quran 4:3.

the other hand, three types exist in the Shi'a laws: regular marriage, purchasing a slave, and a temporary marriage. Amongst Sunni and Shi'a schools of law, the rules that govern marriage vary mildly, yet the overall terms of the contract and the rights and duties of the couple are practically the same.[228]

Based on Quranic rules, some relations by consanguinity, affinity or fostering causes a prohibition to marry; a man may not marry his mother, sisters, daughters, as well as certain women from his wife or ex-wives' families.[229] A woman who suckles anyone else's child sits in the position of his/her mother. Thus the same incest rules for the blood relations apply to the suckled child and her family. For instance, the daughter and son of the wet nurse are considered the child's siblings in case of marriage.[230]

I. Regular Marriage

Spectorsky writes, "ideally a girl or a woman is given in marriage by her guardian. She should be betrothed to a groom who is not closely related to her and is her equal in status, in the presence of witnesses, and she should receive a marriage portion."[231] Each of these elements is a topic of discussion in legal literature. A regular marriage contract has several essential elements, which included: absence of impediments, a formal formula, the consent of parties, the existence of a guardian from the woman's agnatic kin, witnesses, and marriage portion.

---

[228] For a summary account of marriage in classical Islamic jurisprudence, see Kecia Ali, "Marriage in Classical Islamic Jurisprudence: A Survey of Doctrines," in *The Islamic Marriage Contract: Case Studies in Islamic Family Law,* ed. Asifa Quraishi and Frank E. Vogel (Cambridge, MA: Islamic Legal Studies Program, Harvard Law School, 2008).

[229] Quran 4: 22,23.

[230] Wakin, "Family Law."

[231] Susan A. Spectorsky, *Women in Classical Islamic Law a Survey of the Sources* (Leiden: Brill, 2010), 63.

Guardianship. The institution of guardianship is as old as the time that women themselves became a resource for their sexual and their reproductive capacities.[232] Muslim jurists just canonized this salient characteristic of patriarchal family order. Briefly, the male heads of clan, tribe or family were responsible for the legal affairs of the women, the children, and the slaves of his community. Although there are no obvious signs of confirmation about the necessity of guardianship in Quranic commands or the prophet's conduct, however, there is indirect support in the aims of some *hadiths* and implications of some Quranic words, Muslim Jurists confirmed guardianship as a requirement in the marriage of the daughters and in the numerous aspects of wives' lives. *Ibn Abi Shayba* reports from Aisha, who narrates from the prophet, that a marriage is void without the presence or the agreement of a guardian.[233] However, those *hadith* collections also narrated other historical incidents from the life of the prophet that imply the consent of the bride should be maintained, no matter if she is a virgin or widow. "There were lengthy discussions among jurists about whether a father must consult his virgin daughter before giving her in marriage, whether he should do so even if he does not have to, or whether he should do so once she has reached puberty."[234]

It can be implied from these discussions that marrying off a daughter without her consent was an already socially constructed and prevailing tradition, which jurists could not resist or ban, even though, as Spectorsky reports, the jurists did know the prophet's sayings and traditions regarding the subject.

Age of marriage. The Quran did not stipulate a specific age for marriage, yet it

---

[232] Lerner, *The Creation of Patriarchy*, 212-29.

[233] Spectorsky, *Women in Classical Islamic Law*, 64-65.

[234] Ibid., 66.

synchronizes the time of marriage with maturity (sound judgment) and ability to manage their property. "And test the orphans [in their abilities] until they reach marriageable age. Then if you perceive in them sound judgment, release their property to them."[235] No legal system or civil law in Muslim countries gives a nine-year old daughter the custody of any possession. Based on a *hadith* from Aisha, Muslim jurists set the legal age of marriage, most of the time, at either puberty or nine years for girls and fifteen for boys.[236] Some schools of law do not require puberty for marrying off a girl. "In a famous tradition on the authority of Aisha, she says: The prophet married me when I was six or seven and had intercourse with me when I was nine years of age."[237] Like guardianship, marrying off a minor child had been in existence in other ancient legal systems, and as Ali indicates, despite many disagreements upon specific points of law about minor marriage, there was a broader social agreement over the legitimacy of marrying off a minor in Islamic law. The jurists discussed every detail of marrying off a minor child; for instance, whether a minor child can abrogate the marriage after coming to puberty or not.[238] But they did not discuss the legitimacy of the practice in the first place, which indicates the social acceptance of the practice.

Ideal wife. In her paper, "Search of an Ideal Spouse," Nadia Maria El Cheikh examines two old *adab* books in Muslim literature, *Uyun al-akhbar* of Ibn Qutayba (d. 276/889) and *al-Iqd al-farid* of Ibn Abd Rabbih (d. 328/940). The author found common features regarding an ideal wife in both works, including beauty, virginity, and modesty/passivity. The latter feature was

---

[235] Quran 4:6.

[236] There are still other accounts that set the age twelve for marriage of a girl.

[237] Spectorsky, *Women in Classical Islamic Law*, 64.

[238] Ali, *Marriage and Slavery*, 30.

explained such as a perfectly disciplined and obedient wife. *Al-Iqd* describes a beautiful woman with the following words: "the smooth feet, the copious legs, and the rounded knees, all the way to the arms and hands, the red cheeks, the black hair, and the large eyes."[239]

Social rank. According to the principal of *kafa'a*, or equality, the prospective husband must be equal to the wife's father in several respects, depending on the school of law, including family status, occupation, and financial resources.[240] In Muslim jurisprudence, the choosing of an appropriate bridegroom has been discussed in terms of *Kafa'a*[241] and its most common components are lineage, social class, wealth and piety. This reflects the fact that in the formative period of Islam the victorious Arab Muslims adopted the idea of Arab superiority, despite the principal that all Muslims theoretically are equal before God.[242] However, Wakin believes, this ruling functions for dissolution of an unwanted marriage, "either by the minor bride when she comes of age, or by the guardian of the adult bride if she happens to have concluded her own unsuitable marriage."[243]

Marriage contract. Governed by a set of rules, a marriage contract in Islam is similar to a trade transaction in which the woman along with her guardian is the seller; the man is the purchaser, while the object of sale is the woman's sexuality. It is accompanied by a designated

---

[239] Nadia Maria Cheikh, "In Search for the Ideal Spouse," *Journal of the Economic and Social History of the Orient* 45, no. 2 (2002): 188-89.

[240] Wakin, "Family Law."

[241] See Yvon Linant de Bellefonds, "Kaf□a," in *Encyclopedia of Islam*, 2012, accessed October 15, 2016, http://referenceworks.brillonline.com/entries/ encyclopaedia-of-islam-2/kafaa-SIM_3772?s.num=84&s.start=80.

[242] Spectorsky, *Women in Classical Islamic Law*, 76.

[243] Wakin, "Family Law."

formula of offering and acceptance, two witnesses, and a specific amount of money or property

as dower.[244] "Most Muslim jurists required women to be represented by a male guardian, who

accepted an offer[245] for the woman from a suitor of appropriate class and status."[246] The bride

had to give her consent for the marriage contract to be valid.[247] Mir-Hussaini writes,

> Classical *figh* texts define marriage as a contract of exchange with fixed terms and
> uniform legal effects. Modeled after the contract of sale, the essential components of the
> contract are: the offer by the woman or her guardian, the acceptance by the man, and the
> payment of dower, a sum of money or any valuable that the husband pays or undertakes
> to pay to the bride before or after consummation.[248]

The pre-Islamic tradition of the exchange of the marriage portion – that is, that the

bridegroom's family paid the bride's family for the dowry (that the bride brought to the

bridegroom family in the first place) – was changed by certain Quranic teachings. According to

the Quran, the groom must provide the bride with a marriage portion.[249] The bride herself is

entitled to marriage portion while she keeps her right of inheritance from her agnate family, her

husband, and her children whom she survived.[250] If the marriage portion has not been stipulated

at the time of marriage, still the husband cannot divorce her without offering her a divorce gift.[251]

---

[244] Ziba Mir-Hosseini, "The Construction Of Gender in Islamic Legal Thought and Strategies for Reform," *Hawwa* 1, no.1 (2003): 4-5.

[245] About this statement of Lapidus I will discuss in the comparison section of marriage.

[246] Lapidus, *Islamic Societies, 186.*

[247] Ibid.

[248] Mir-Hosseini, "The Construction of Gender," 4-5.

[249] Quran, 4:4, 24; 5:5.

[250] Spectorsky, *Women in Classical Islamic Law,* 30.

[251] Quran, 2:236.

Another salient feature of Islamic marriage contract, set by jurisprudence, is the concept of "obedience" as the primary and major duty of a wife. As Tucker states, "The *Sharia* defined marriage as a relationship of reciprocity, in which a man owed his wife material support and a woman owed her husband obedience."[252] The Islamic jurists first made the husband financially responsible for her maintenance, even though she can maintain herself, and then tied the husband's responsibility for her maintenance with her responsibility to be obedient to him.

Polygamy. Multiple marriages are permitted to men, who may have up to four wives at the same time.[253] With some interpretation of the specific verses of the Quran, Muslim jurists added unlimited concubines for a man in the Sunni and Shi'a jurisprudences and unlimited temporary marriage for him in the Shi'a family law.

II. Marriage to Slaves

Marriage to slaves, in both sexes, was formed as a legal institution, which has been distinguished from concubinage in Islam. Here, in addition to the consent of the couple, which is mandatory in a regular marriage, the consent of the owner of the slave partner should be maintained. After marriage, if the slave partner is sold, the new master has the right either to confirm or reject the marriage agreement. A married female slave could not be her master's concubine after marriage with another man. Children from mixed unions are free while children whose parents are both slaves "share the servile status of the parents."[254] Although a man could have sex with his own female slave, he could not marry her as long as he owned her. In order to

---

[252] Tucker, "Gender and Islamic History," 41.

[253] Quran, 4:3.

[254] Hamid Algar, "Barda and Barda-Dari vi. Regulations Governing Slavery in Islamic Jurisprudence," in *Encyclopedia Iranica*, 1988, accessed October 15, 2016, http:// www.iranic aonline.org/articles/barda-vi.

marry his own female slave, the owner has to free her first.[255] To marry a female slave, a man

must not be her owner, meaning; the woman should be another's slave.

III. Temporary Marriage, *mut'a*

Although there are important differences in their sectarian doctrines between the twelver

Shi'a[256] and Sunni Islam, they exhibit a few differences in their family law. The institution of

temporary marriage is one of those rare cases in which they differ. This type of marriage, has not

been fully accepted by the mainstream Sunni legal schools as a legal marriage; Murata writes,

> The Sunni authorities agree that the Prophet at certain points permitted *mut'a* during his
> lifetime, but they maintain that in the end he prohibited it completely. In contrast, the
> Shi'a maintain that the Prophet did not ban it, and they cite numerous *hadith* from Sunni
> as well as Shi'a sources to prove this.[257]

Mut'a in Arabic means "enjoyment, pleasure." Its meaning shows its purpose is different

from a regular marriage. Nevertheless, it is contracted like regular marriage with similar

components including formula, consent of couple, witnesses, and marriage portion. The two

types of marriage differ in the time period of marriage, which is stipulated for a limited period of

time, and in the legal rights of the spouses. Temporary marriage could last from a few minutes to

ninety-nine years depending on the couple's decision in the contract. There is no divorce in

temporary marriage, since the couple becomes separated from each other by the expiration of the

stipulated time period, or else by the man's forgiveness of the remaining time to the woman.

There is no such right for the wife to end the marriage unless it is mentioned in the contract.

---

[255] Ali, *Marriage and Slavery,* 167.

[256] Shi'a itself has different branches, and the twelvers have been considered the largest
in number and the most influential in theology and jurisprudence.

[257] Sachiko, Murata, *Temporary Marriage (Mut'a) in Islamic Law* (Qum, Iran: Ansariyan
Publications, 1987), accessed April 21, 2015, https://www.al-islam.org/ printpdf/ book/ export/
html/11245.

Also, a temporary wife was not "legally entitled to financial support, not even if she is
pregnant."[258] Although a temporary wife must obey her husband, the degree of her obedience is
limited and is not as complete as that of a permanent wife. Khomeini in his "Book of Exegesis"
states, she may exercise her will as long as her activities do not interfere with her husband's
rights, specifically, his right to sexual enjoyment; otherwise, her activities are forbidden.[259] A
temporary wife is not legally entitled to financial support, shelter and inheritance from her
temporary husband. However, her children are legitimate children of the temporary husband.[260]
But it is noteworthy that accepting the legitimacy of the child is totally based on the husband's
will. If he denies his paternity, even without any evidence, the child will be abandoned without
custody and alimony.[261]

IV. Concubinage

A man has sexual access to his female slave as long as she is not married to someone
else. The only exception is "he owns both a mother and her daughter, or two sisters, he can
choose only one of the two for his bed."[262] This is different from marrying someone else's slave
and has been regulated as a master-slave relationship. This relationship does not follow marriage
rules and rights, except in case of offspring. The child produced by concubinage is free and
legitimate. In most juridical discussion a concubine with legitimate child should not be sold and

---

[258] Ibid.

[259] Shahla Haeri, *Law of Desire: Temporary Marriage in Shi'i Iran* (Syracuse: Syracuse
University Press, 2014), 59.

[260] Ibid., 49-72.

[261] Muratr, "Mut'a."

[262] Algar, "Barda and Barda-dari."

she is free after her owner's death.[263] Muslim jurists have a precedent from the life story of the

prophet who emancipated his slave and married her. However, in spite of Sunni affirmation of

the ruling, in some cases, Shi'a scholars allowed the sale of such a concubine.[264] As it was

explicitly mentioned earlier, a concubine partner has no legal rights except that of what a slave is

entitled to in Islamic jurisprudence.

V. Mixed Marriage

A Muslim cannot marry a none-Muslim with the exception of a Muslin man who may

marry a woman from the people of the book, usually meaning Jews and Christians.[265] There is

one verse that allows Muslim men to marry women from other religions.[266] However The Quran

is silent about inter-religions matrimony for Muslim women, while Jurists prohibited this kind of

marriage. Ali states,

> The vast majority of texts assume free men's right to take slave concubines and never
> raise the issue of female owners taking male concubines, even to reject it as
> impermissible. A similar silence obtains on the question of a Muslim woman marrying a
> non-Muslim man. Although more or less universally forbidden, this prohibition on
> Muslim women's intermarriage was taken for granted; most do not bother to explain.[267]

Marriage Law: An Indicator of Cultural Continuity

Based on some clear Quranic statements, specific Zoroastrian/Sasanian types of wedlock

were prohibited by Muslim law, including Next-of-Kin marriage and Proxy marriage. Contrary

---

[263] Joseph Schacht, "Umm al-Walad," in *Encyclopaedia of Islam, Second Edition*, Brill Online, 2015, http://referenceworks.brillonline.com/entries/encyclopaedia-of-islam-2/umm-al-walad- COM_1290.

[264] Algar, "Barda and Barda-dari."

[265] Ali, "Marriage in Classical Islamic Jurisprudence, " 86.

[266] Quran, 5:5.

[267] Ali, *Marriage and Slavery*, 177.

to Zoroastrian jurisprudence, in which a man could marry any woman, even their mothers, daughters and sisters, Islamic Law placed restrictions on marriage partnership. Eligible persons have been restricted on different bases notably blood relation, relation by marriage, and relation by fostering. The Quranic verses of 4:22,23 designate the individuals that one cannot marry as first-degree female family members, aunts and grandmothers, as well as mother- and sisters-in-law and many others that were identified elsewhere in the Quran. As a result, next of kin marriage became completely forbidden. In addition, the Quran 33:4-5 asserts that a proxy child is not the same as the biological child in terms of rights and responsibilities, which renders a proxy marriage useless for its purposes.

Nevertheless, according to Lapidus, "Late antique marriage practices and sexual morality did not significantly change in early Muslim communities."[268] Christian Bartholomae goes one step further and states that the Sasanian marriage was very similar to the marriage in the Islamic world.[269]

I. Principal Marriage

The two traditions are different in the kin relations that prohibited marriage, the importance of virginity, and the legal consequence of second marriage for a woman. As it was mentioned before, based on consanguinity, affinity or fostering, there are a number of people that a Muslims could not marry, whereas there is no such prohibition in Zoroastrianism. In the Sasanian tradition, virginity played a crucial role in a principal marriage. Usually, a non-virgin bride was not eligible for a principal marriage, and consequently for both she and her children, also the right to inherit from the husband. Islamic law did not pose such conditions for a

---

[268] Lapidus, *Islamic Societies*, 186.

[269] Bartholomae, *Zan dar Hoghough*, 51.

principal marriage or the law of inheritance. However, traditionally, virginity is still considered a

necessary condition for the first marriage. It was not written in the law books or marriage

contracts that the principal wife should be virgin, yet it was a common sense, manifested in the

judicial debates. In Islamic societies, the importance of virginity has been reflected on the

guardian's exclusive rights over virgin daughter. In Zoroastrian law, marriage of a non-virgin

woman was categorized as □*akar*□*h,* in which wife and her children lacked the advantages of a

principal marriage, economically and legally. Second marriage in Islamic Law has been

considered a pious, recommended, and favored act, and not just an Iranian old tradition,

shameful and almost unforgiveable.

Guardianship. The regulation of the family law in both traditions maintained the

necessity and the authorization of a guardian in a marriage. The authority of a guardian in

Islamic law particularly regarding marrying off a daughter, covered a vast area of legal cases,

from the legitimacy of marrying her off when she is still a minor, to separating her from her

husband when she had chosen an improper husband by herself, both without her consent.[270]

Zoroastrian texts confirm the legitimacy of marrying off a minor child by his/her guardian.[271]

Some legal maxims containing similar subjects in these two traditions follow similar formats or

expression. For instance, regarding the authority or importance of a guardian in marriage,

Musannaf of Ibn Abi Shayba reports, "Aisha said: The prophet said: 'There can be no marriage

---

[270] Susan A. Spectorskey, *Chapters in Marriage and Divorce: Responses of Ibn Hanbal and Ibn Rahwayh,* (Austin: University of Texas Press, 1993), 63-64.

[271] Mansour Shaki, "Divorce: In the Parthian and Sasanian periods," in *Encyclopedia Iranica,* 1995, accessed October 15, 2016, http://www.iranicaonline.org/articles/divorce#pt2.

without a guardian…'"[272] MHD 4.9-10 states, "Divorce takes effect only when accompanied

with dissolution of the guardianship.[273] About the origin of the Islamic maxim Schacht states,

> The opinion that there is no valid marriage without a *wali* [guardian] found its first
> expression in the alleged decision of Umar ibn-Abdul Aziz that such marriages must be
> dissolved. This is no doubt later than the Caliphate of Umar ibn-Abdul Aziz and dates
> only from the second century A.H. it was held in Iraq, Medina, and Mecca. Projected
> back to Ali, Umar, and Ibn-Abbas, and finally ascribed to the Prophet, on the authority of
> Aisha and of other companions; the traditions which put it into the mouth of the Prophet
> appear only from Shafi'i onwards. The legal Maxim was coined at this later stage. Abu
> Yusuf, having held an opinion near to that of abu-Hanifa at first, adopted this doctrine,
> Shaybani held it, Shafi'i supported it with a brilliant systematic argument."[274]

It is hard to prove the Persian ancestry of Abu-Hanifa or semi-Iranian culture of Iraq itself had

something to do with the similarity of the maxims, that is no marriage/divorce without

guardian/guardianship. However, it deserves to be considered.

Age of marriage. According to Islamic jurisprudence, the legal age of puberty is nine for

girls and fifteen for boys. The age of marriage may vary a little based on the jurists' variable

opinions. However, it does not fluctuate for girls outside the ages of nine to twelve. As

aforementioned, in Zoroastrian texts it is the same. In both traditions, the marriage contract can

be concluded years before the actual marriage. Marrying off a minor child had been in existence

in other ancient legal systems, and as Ali indicates, despite many disagreements on the specific

points of law about minor marriage, there was a broader social agreement over the legitimacy of

marrying off a minor in Islamic law.[275] In both traditions, there are debates regarding the

---

[272] Spectorsky, *Women in Classical Islamic Law*, 64.

[273] Perikhanian, MHD, 35.

[274] Joseph Schacht, *The Origins of Muhammadan Jurisprudence* (Oxford: Oxford
University Press, 1967), 183, accessed October 15, 2016, http://hdl.handle.net/2027/heb. 00936.

[275] Ali, *Marriage and Slavery in Early Islam*, 30.

possibility of divorce when the minor daughter reaches puberty. The majority of jurists, in both

traditions, believe that the minor daughter cannot dissolve her marriage.

Ideal wife. Cheikh believes that these descriptions of female beauty belong to the

"Ancient Arab canon of beauty;"[276] nonetheless, as it was evident before, the beauty in Persia

was nearly the same in such terms like black hair, white skin, and large black eyes. The concept

of absolute obedience before the husband also is common, as well as moral characteristics like

chastity and modesty. In support of the idea that these female beauty norms may originally

belong to Persia, it is noteworthy to mention that Ibn Qutaibeh was of Persian ancestry and spent

his lifetime in Persia. Also, even though Ibn Abd Rabbih was an Andalusian writer, as Sheikh

indicates, *Al-Iqd* [his work], is drawn from the works of Ibn al-Muqaffa, al-Jahiz, Ibn Qutayba,

al-Mubarrad and other earlier works of "eastern" [Iran and Iraq] origins."[277] Even with this in

view, it is hard to imply that these norms of "ideal spouse" originally belonged to Persians

[Zoroastrian/Sasanian]. The preference of a beautiful wife over an ugly one has its rational point,

considering the fact that it is the prospective husband or his family's choice. Furthermore, a

modest and obedient wife is a strong demand and nonnegotiable element of a patriarchal family

structure. Nonetheless, it is acceptable to conclude that these resemblances illustrate the

continuity of cultural norms and values in the region, particularly Iran and Iraq. This conclusion

would be more convincing, if we consider the ontological perspective of the Quran regarding

marriage. Addressing an ideal marriage, Muslim scripture [the Quran] puts the verses like the

following as norm: God "created for you mates from among yourselves, that you may dwell in

---

[276] Cheikh, "In Search for the Ideal Spouse," 189.

[277] Ibid., 185.

tranquility with them, and God has put love and mercy between you.[278] Obviously, a family

structure based on tranquility, love, and mercy between spouses is totally different from the one

that is based on modesty and obedience of one party before the other. With respect to modesty

and obedience in literature and jurisprudence, perhaps these patriarchal family norms exceeded

the original teachings of Islam.

Social rank. Marriage within the same social rank in the Sasanian law has been

maintained by their class system. Based on the Quranic statements, a male believer is a suitable

partner for a female believer, regardless of wealth or social class. Thus, Muslim jurists regulated

the "same class marriage" under the topic of *Kafa'a* (equality); in other words, the husband

should be in the same social rank as the wife's father.[279]

After the conquest of Iran, Arabs held social and political superiority over non-Arabs for more

than two centuries; as a result, non-Arabs could not marry an Arab woman. As it was said before,

Persians did not give their daughter to other nations, a practice that Arabs imitated when they

conquered Persia, in spite of the egalitarian teaching of the Quran.

Marriage contract. Contrary to the trade nature of the Muslim marriage contract,

Mazaheri believes Zoroastrian marriage is far from being a kind of trade.[280] Nevertheless,

consider the following facts: the daughter is transferred to the husband's family and all legal

connections, such as guardianship and inheritance, between the daughter and her agnate family

are cut. Her father receives the dowry/marriage portion from the husband's family and gives the

---

[278] The Quran 30: 21.

[279] Not all the jurisprudential schools are the same; for example, Shi'a jurisprudence,
which was formed in fifth/eleventh century, held that the principal of *Kafa'a* is maintained just
by faith.

[280] Mazaheri, *Khanevadeh Irani*, 73.

daughter her share from the family's wealth, given there is no future right of inheritance for her. The share she brings goes under the control of the husband's family and, as will be discussed, even at the time of divorce the daughter usually cannot claim her dowry. I suggest the Zoroastrian marriage contract fully functioned as a trade contract in which a father gives up his rights and responsibilities over his daughter and bestow them upon whomever had paid for her.

On the other hand, the women's rights and responsibilities, announced by the Quran,[281] has tied the Muslim jurists' hands to produce such a document that can entirely cut legal connections between a daughter and her paternal family. Therefore they limited the sale to just buying her sexuality not her whole existence.[282] While the marriage contract could not give the husband full control over his wife's activities, this control is maintained through jurisprudential speculations. Muslim jurists limited the wife's mobility based on the argument that a wife cannot do anything that would restrain her husband's access to her sexuality that he has bought through the marriage contract. Thus for instance, she is prohibited to leave the husband's home without his permission, even if she is going to visit her parents. Mir-Hosseini writes,

> Among the default rights of the husband is his power to control his wife's movements and her "excess piety." She needs his permission to leave the house, to take up employment, or to engage in fasting or forms of worship other than what is obligatory (for example, the fast of Ramadan), because such acts may violate the husband's right of 'unhampered sexual access.[283]

Putting the position of a husband elevated over the wife, or perhaps, saving his dignity during the process of "offer and acceptance," interestingly, formally in both traditions it is the

---

[281] Including her legal entity and financial rights.

[282] Ziba Mir-Hosseini, "Sexuality and Inequality: The Marriage Contract and Muslim Legal Tradition," in *Sexuality in Muslim Contexts: Restrictions and Resistance* (London: Zed Books, 2012), 128-32.

[283] Ibid., 128.

guardian of the wife who offers his daughter, and it is the husband who accepts the wife, while practically the husband and his family is the one who choose a girl and ask her father for her hand. Macuch in her commentary on the third clause of the "Pahlavi Model marriage contract" states, "Several legal formulae are used in this clause. The first one 'by request and transfer' refers to the indispensable formal act by which the prospective groom asks the father or guardian of the prospective bride for her hand in marriage and is accepted by the father who transfers his daughter into the lineage of the husband."[284] According to this passage, the request is from the groom. However, translation of article five by both Yakubovich and Macuch indicates that the request is from the father of the bride and the acceptance is from the side of the groom: "And the bridegroom accepted her from her father in this manner that …"[285]

Like Sasanian tradition, in Islam, the request is from father of the bride and the acceptance is from the side of the groom. Lapidus states, "Late antique marriage practices and sexual morality did not significantly change in early Muslim communities. Generally, an Islamic marriage is a contract between the bride (who makes a marriage offer) and a groom (who accepts the offer and pays the dower) in the presence of two witnesses."[286] Ali writes: "it is standard practice for the offer of marriage to be made from the bride's party to the groom's party, though this sequence is not a condition for the validity of the marriage according to Hanafi, Maliki, Shafi'i, and Jafari doctrine."[287] The arrangement of offer/acceptance in the marriage contract

---

[284] Macuch, "Pahlavi Model Marriage Contract," 195.

[285] Macuch, "Pahlavi Model Marriage Contract," 190; Yakubovich, "The Marriage Contract.

[286] Lapidus, *Islamic Societies*, 186.

[287] Ali, "Marriage in Classical Islamic Jurisprudence," 13.

formula, even today, is the same as it was in the formative period of jurisprudential schools: offer from the bride's party and acceptance from the groom's party.

In the Islamic tradition, marriage could be concluded by a verbal formula, while a few centuries earlier the Sasanians had a written document for a marriage contract. Even though the Muslim tradition also gradually changed to a written contract, the older tradition of a verbal formula was preserved in the jurisprudence. Perhaps the advanced religious institution of the Sasanians demanded a written document. However, it is possible that at remote regions of the empire a verbal formula was practiced and relied more on the witnesses. Both traditions used specific statements for marriage and divorce. Furthermore, in the Islamic tradition most of the transactions happen with the presence of two witnesses while, based on codex MK the witnesses are three in Zoroastrianism.

Both traditions proclaim that the consent of the bride is mandatory for her marriage, however, as it was discussed before, in both traditions, the discussions regarding the marriage of a minor child, particularly a daughter, implies the father has absolute authority to marry off his virgin and minor daughter without her consent.[288]

About financial transactions in a marriage contract, two parties who contract the marriage and are involved in the process of give-and-take are the guardian of the wife on one side and the husband, usually accompanied by his own father or head of the family on the other side. Financial activities related to a marriage contract was a matter between those men and the wife

---

[288] Spectorsky, *Chapters on Marriage and Divorce*, 9-13; Ali, "Marriage in Classical Islamic Jurisprudence," 17-19; Spectorsky, *Women in Classical Islamic Law,* 63; Behramgore Tahmuras Anklesaria, trans. *The Pahlavi Rivayat of Adur-Farnbag*, Avesta -- Zoroastrian Archives, 1938, aaccessed October 15, 2016, http://www.avesta.org/mp/ adurfarn.html.

[289] Lerner, *The Creation of Patriarchy*, 107; Macuch, The Pahlavi Marriage Contract, 197-98.

just announces her consent to participate in their arrangement. The party who offers the girl is entitled to the marriage portion (dower) and the one who accepts her would be her new guardian as well as the manager of her share from her father's possession.[289] This kind of arrangement was the old tradition of the ancient world, and its traces could still be observed in 19th century CE European family laws. The Quranic rulings reformed this practice,[290] seemingly to improve the financial and, consequentially, social independence of women.[291] However, the resistance of the old tradition modified the Quranic ruling through jurisprudential activities, aiming to restrict women's mobility, as I explained in the marriage contract section.

Polygamy. Following the Quranic verse at Q 4:3, Muslim jurists sanctioned up to four wives for a man. However they did pardon unlimited concubines and temporary marriage.[292] These rulings usually regulated for the advantage of kings and elite men. Metz in his excellent work, "The Renaissance of Islam," reports, in the forth/tenth century, "All reports and stories suggest that the middle class was monogamous."[293] Sasanian texts did not support polygamy and further condemned the layman for having more than one wife, unless the principal wife was barren. It seems as though some characteristics of the Sasanian family unit acted against polygamy. For instance, Sasanian extended families used to live in their undividable lands and had strong ties to the land and its resources. Polygamy could be a source of conflict between the children of the multiple wives and a serious damage to the sedentary life of the kinship group.

---

[290] "Give the women [upon marriage] their [bridal] gifts graciously," Quran 4:4.

[291] Lapidus, *Islamic Societies*, 210-13.

[292] Temporary marriage has been not supported in Sunni Islam.

[293] Adam Mez, *The Renaissance of Islam* (Patna, India: Jubilee Print. & Pub. House, 1937), 363.

Remarriage of widows or divorcees prevailed in the Arabian Peninsula's tradition before Islam and the new religion had no difficulty with it either. For instance, although the multiple marriages of Khadija, the first wife of Muhammad, may be considered as a pre-Islamic tradition, the multiple marriages of the respectful companion of the prophet Muhammad, Asma bint Umais, are entirely Islamic. Asma married three times; all of her husbands were the prominent disciples of the prophet: namely, the distinguished cousin of the prophet, Ja'far ibn Abu Talib; the first Caliph, Abu Bakr; and the fourth Caliph, Ali ibn Abu Talib.[294]

Nevertheless, the practice was condemned by Sasanian tradition in which a wife was considered her husband's consort even after his death. After a few centuries Muslims in Mesopotamia turned against the practice too. Mez writes,

> Though sanctioned by law, remarriage of widows was highly disapproved by custom. A story of the 3rd/9th century mentions the writing of a letter to a friend whose mother remarries, when a widow, as the most difficult of tasks. He solves the difficulty thus: Fate follows a course different from man's desire. May God who determines his servant's destiny, grand you her death for the grave is the noblest of husbands. In a similar strain wrote Khwarizmi (d. 303/1003) to the historian Miskawaihi when his widowed mother remarried: before I could have prayed God to keep her alive for thy sake; but now, I pray that He may take her away as speedily as possible, for the grave is a better husband and death a more coveted honor. Thank God, the want of dutifulness and affection is on her side, not yours.[295]

II. Marriage Without a Guardian

Marriage of a girl without the consent of her guardian has been discussed in the law books of both traditions, as aforementioned. In both traditions, this kind of marriage has

---

[294] Muḥammad Ibn Sa'ad, *The Women of Madina*, translated by Aisha Abd-ur-Rahman Bewley (London: Ta-Ha, 1997), 198-99.

[295] Mez, *The Renaissance of Islam*, 364.

culturally been condemned.[296] However, legally the daughter could not be rejected from all her

financial rights. Divorcees and widows from low class families might marry without guardians as

well.

III. Temporary Marriage

This thesis brought forward the works of some prominent scholars about Zoroastrian

family law. None of them, except Macuch, used the term "temporary marriage," since there is no

such term in the Zoroastrian legal texts. Macuch interestingly coined the term in Zoroastrian

studies and in her article, "The Function of Temporary Marriage in the Context of Sasanian

Family Law," arguing that all forms of the Zoroastrian marriages could be concluded on a

temporary basis.[297] Comparing temporary marriage in two traditions, Macuch concludes,

> In the context of Sasanian family law, temporary marriage has an important function and
> consequently its logical place in the underlying pattern of kinship and marriage… This
> practice was in fact strange, and alien to the concept of Muslim marriage and
> tremendously controversial. Macuch further concludes and assumes that "temporary
> marriage is in fact one of the age old institutions of Iranian law that survived the Muslim
> invasion of custom and had been practiced for many centuries."[298]

Macuch names the Shi'a Temporary marriage as "a legal outlet for sexual needs."

Temporary marriage is often regarded "outside Shi'a circles only as another form of

prostitution."[299] I found Macuch's argument convincing, because the historical reports illustrate

---

[296] All over the world, even today, a woman with a male relative who considers himself
as a guardian or responsible for her, cannot freely come into contact with a strange man. See
AIUSA's Women's Human Rights Program website at www.amnestyusa.org/ women regarding
"honor killing."

[297] Macuch, "The Pahlavi Model Marriage Contracts," 587.

[298] Macuch, "The Function of Temporary Marriage," 594-595.

[299] Ibid., 586.

"In ancient Mesopotamia adultery was an offence against a husband but not against a wife."[300] Thus no punishment for a husband in case of extra-marital affairs, while the woman shall be killed.[301] Since sex out of marriage, in the Quran, has equal punishment for both sexes, the establishment of a legal institution for the male "sexual needs" had been required.

Nonetheless, I believe some elements amongst her assumptions are still missing. I suggest that the temporary marriage *in* Shi's context means sexual advantage without legal responsibility. It is comparable to some sort of auxiliary marriage in the Zoroastrian context where the husband has no legal responsibility over his wife and her children, for instance, marriage with a widow or a divorcee. In those cases there are no legal responsibilities such as maintenance and inheritance for the wife and her children, the same as temporary marriage in Shi's, especially when the husband does not desire to accept the legitimacy of his child produced in a temporary marriage.[302] Furthermore, even though some types of *akar* marriage were concluded permanently, the husband could leave the *akar* wife whenever he wanted and without her consent.[303]

IV. Concubinage

Concubinage, which prevailed in the Sasanian court also survived the Muslim conquest of Iran and had been practiced more than ever in the Abbasid period among both aristocrats and

---

[300] Beth Troy, "Legally Bound: A Study of Women's Legal Status in the Ancient Near East," (Master's thesis, Miami University, 2004), accessed October 15, 2016. https://etd.ohiolink.edu/, 17.

[301] Ibid.

[302] He can deny the legitimacy of the child and for this rejection has not legal obligation, for instance, going through the *li'an* procedure. Murata, "*Mut'a*."

[303] Daryaee, *Sasanian Persia*, 61.

commoners. Baghdad had great slave-markets in which slaves from all around the ancient world were sold. Hassan reports, even free women from Medina or elsewhere through the Empire had themselves sold in Baghdad to enjoy the comfort of the Imperial court and the aristocrats' houses.[304] In the early forth/tenth century, there were upper-class slaves that may be sold privately to the luxurious households.[305]

Based on Muslim *Sharia*, the caliph, like other Muslim men, could have four wives. However they preferred to have none. By the late second century AH, the Abbasid caliphs rarely married free women and preferred concubines. "All the Caliphs of the forth/tenth century were the sons of slave-girls.[306] Nevertheless, as Abbott states, "The seclusion of the harem affected the free-born Arab woman to a greater extent than it did her captive or slave-born sisters."[307]

V. Mixed Marriage

Islamic jurisprudence allowed a Muslim man to marry a non-Muslim woman from 'The People of the Book,' meaning a member of Zoroastrian, Jewish, or Christian faith. A Muslim woman has no such option, same as the Zoroastrian tradition in the Sasanian period. Nevertheless, after the Arab conquest of Iran, Zoroastrian communities banned interfaith marriages for both men and women, so protecting the vulnerable, and under-attack Zoroastrian faith.[308] The child produced by such a marriage, even though the father was a Zoroastrian, belonged to the non-Zoroastrian community. REA 42.2 asserts, "If a man of the good religion

---

[304] Hasan, *Tarikh.e. Syasi*, 353.

[305] Mez, *The Renaissance of Islam*, 160.

[306] Ibid., 364.

[307] Abbott, *Two Queens of Baghdad*, 8.

[308] Choksy, "Zoroastrians in Muslim Iran," 24.

copulates with a woman of another religion and she becomes pregnant as a result of this

copulation, then for granting offspring to [a member of] another religion the *tanapuhl*[309] sin is

prescribed."[310]

Conclusion

A survey of Sasanian marriage indicates the Iranians' unique way of maintaining their

ontological view of the concept of marriage and family order, as well as their strong tendency to

keep the family's wealth intact, mainly of vast lands. Some of their marriage customs vanished

once their political/economic status and interests changed while the rest inspired the new

civilization, which has been built on their ruins.

An answer to the question of why some Sasanian traditions had strong effects on the

Islamic jurisprudence while the rest left no traces was the specific rulings of the Quran itself.

Another answer, I suggest, would be due to this fact that such traditions may not have been

profoundly or extensively practiced in the first place. Thus, such traditions could not last when

they lost the Sasanian's institutional religious propaganda at the advent of the Islamic era.

---

[309] A *tanapuhl* sin prevents the soul from crossing the "Bridge of the Separator."

[310] Choksy, "Zoroastrians in Muslim Iran," 24.

CHAPTER 4

DIVORCE IN TWO TRADITIONS

Broadly speaking, in the ancient Near East divorce was a unilateral act that allowed husband and wife to dissolve their marriage. However, even though in theory both parties could perform divorce, in practice many systems in the region "precluded the wife's right to divorce."[311] Troy implies from her research "nine times out of ten, men retained the sole power to divorce their wives."[312] Legally, divorce took place by a verbal declaration in front of the wife and a few witnesses. Financial transactions were a part of divorce, imposed by the society's general law or by mutual agreement within the marriage contract, including her dowry and/or settlement price. Indeed these varied by systems. "Some systems imposed financial penalties by operation of law, although they varied in severity from the amount of the "bride-price" where there were no children, up to the whole of the husband's property where there were children, to nothing."[313] If a wife abandoned the husband's house, she deserted empty-handed and might face further legal punishments, even death. Observing the ancient law systems, divorce meant a huge degradation for a woman. She not only lost her social status as the mistress of the house but she also faced economic hardship, unless she had a wealthy, powerful, and supportive agnate family who could retrieve her dowry and divorce settlement. In Iran, before the Sasanians, the low-class, divorced women could not seek another husband until the death of her previous husband. "Adultery was a serious offense by the wife against her husband. Called the 'great sin' in a

---

[311] Raymond Westbrook, Gary M. Beckman, *A History of Ancient Near Eastern Law* (Leiden: Brill, 2003), 48.

[312] Troy, *Legally Bound*, 39.

[313] Westbrook, *A History of Ancient Near Eastern law,* 49.

87

number of societies, it was regarded in some way as analogous to treason. It gave the husband a broad discretion in punishing his wife, ranging from death through mutilation to divorce with confiscation of all her property."[314]

Sasanian Divorce

In the Sasanian civil and canon law, only divorcing a principal wife has been discussed, since other types of marriage maintained no rights for a wife, legally or economically. Traditionally, women could not initiate divorce. However, upper-class women could initiate divorce as a part of their class privilege.[315] Termination of marriage may also happen without divorce. For instance, ending a proxy marriage does not require divorce, and once a son had been begotten, the proxy marriage could be terminated without divorce.[316] Unless there was a contract or promises, a *čakar* wife also has no right to claim property, food or provision,[317] and divorcing her did not require her consent.

I. Principal Divorce

According to Zoroastrian law, in theory, both husband and wife could initiate divorce and they might be divorced by the consent of the other party.[318] However women, depending on their status and age, could ask and be granted a divorce. While it was very hard for commoners to divorce or to remarry even after the death of their husbands, the upper class women had much

---

[314] Ibid., 77.

[315] Shaki, "Divorce."

[316] Shaki, "Family Law."

[317] Safa-Isfehani, REA, 53.

[318] Safa-Isfehani, REA, 49; Daryaee, *Sasanian Persia*, 61.

more say.[319] For instance, according to PRA, a girl who married at the age of nine could not turn away from that marriage when she reached fifteen.

> Q: If a daughter of nine years gives her in marriage to a man, can she turn away from the contract, when she becomes fifteen years of age, and become the wife of another man? If she turns away from the contract, what is the sin committed by her towards that man? Will she be the wife of independent status of that other man or not?

> A: As I understand: if a girl of nine years has attained to puberty, she cannot give herself in marriage to a man without the consent of a lawful guardian, and turn away from the wifehood of that man; if she turns away, she is a sinner deserving death, after a full year expires thereafter.[320]

The PRA extended the situation to a mature wife as well,

> Q: A woman of mature age, who gives herself in marriage to a man of mature age, turns away from that man, then what is her sin and punishment of sin committed toward that man? Or if the woman says: "I give myself in marriage unto thee," is it lawful if she does not become his wife?

> A: As I understand: if she gave herself in marriage under lawful guardianship, she cannot turn away from that man; and if she turns away, and will not perform the duties of wife towards that man, and turns away without the consent of her husband, she becomes a *tanapuhr* sinner on the spot, and a sinner deserving death after a full year. She will not be his wife; she will become a sinner deserving death after a full year.[321]

Guardianship in divorce. The rule of guardianship in divorce was as important as it is in marriage. Divorce takes effect only when accompanied with dissolution of the guardianship.[322] Usually, the current guardian should dissolve his guardianship and appoint a new guardian for his wife. MHD 4.9-10 states,

> This opinion has been given regarding the dissolution of a marriage, namely that there is no valid divorce without the appointment of a guardian, and according to the procedure in

---

[319] Shaki, "Divorce."

[320] Anklesaria, PRA, chap.14.

[321] Ibid., chap.16.

[322] Shaki, "The Sasanian Matrimonial," 340.

such a case (the following declaration must be made): "let (her) be given (in guardianship to such a one?)."

It is the husband's responsibility to not abandon his wife without a guardian. If that happens, not only has he committed a deadly sin, but also the children from his wife's second marriage would belong to him.

> In one place it is written that if a man divorces his wife and - except for the case where this (woman) receives from him the right of "self-guardianship" - does not transfer the guardianship to anyone, and (it) this woman subsequently enters into a marriage during the lifetime of this man and bears children, then, the children of this woman belong to him who divorced her in this manner. [323]

The new guardian could be the next husband, who also must announce his acceptance of the guardianship.[324] In late Sasanian times, a widow could be her own guardian. It would be not only due to social changes, but also probably because a widow did not need a guardian to conclude a marriage contract for her, since she could not be a principal wife without virginity and dowry. Otherwise, self-guardianship did not change her legal status; for instance, she could not attend court even if she were a self-guardian.

Consent of the other party. In divorce, like marriage, the consent of the wife is necessary unless she has been accused of a grave sin or she is barren. If a man divorces his wife undeservedly or without the agreement of the wife, it is not lawful and it has consequences. The husband commits a deadly sin,[325] and the wife remains as his principal wife.[326] Nevertheless, a

---

[323] Perikhanian, MHD, 33.

[324] Ibid., 35.

[325] Alan Williams, *The Pahlavi Rivayat Accompanying the Dadestan- i- Denig* (Copenhagen: Munksgaard, 1990), 61.

[326] Safa-Isfehani, REA, 51.

husband could divorce his principal wife without her consent if he found her at fault of the sins

that PRDD expressed as a danger to the body or soul.[327] REA, question seven, reports those sins:

> Whore, sorcerer, disobedient; sinfully abstains from copulating with her husband; does
> not abstain from intercourse during her menstrual period; while still in menstruation goes
> through the procedure of a proxy marriage for her husband; she who hides her
> menstruation; she who gives her body to another man; she who commits any deliberate
> sin, which would afflict the body and soul.[328]

In case of barrenness, the Pahlavi legal texts from ninth century CE and MHD from the

late Sasanian period are silent,[329] though generally barrenness was a morally and socially

acceptable reason to marry a second wife. "Since polygamy was allowed in most cases, divorce

for infertility and illness was really a last resort for most men."[330] While the reasons under which

a man can divorce his wife have been carefully discussed, the legal and religious texts have not

mentioned anything about a wife who can divorce her husband. Hjerrild suggests,

> In the first place it is made abundantly plain here that women have so many claims to
> legal protection that divorce from them cannot be obtained without good and sufficient
> reason and evidence. Hence a woman is a person in her own right. Her consent is
> necessary for divorce. On the other hand, we find no list of grounds justifying a woman's
> application for divorce. Valid grounds for divorce without the wife's consent are found in
> varieties of religious uncleanliness.[331]

Still, there is a way that a principal "immaculate" wife might be divorced against her will.

According to the Sasanian tradition and Zoroastrian Law, the husband had the authority to offer

---

[327] Williams, PRDD, 61.

[328] Safa-Isfehani, REA, 49.

[329] Shaki, "Divorce."

[330] Beth Troy, "Legally Bound," 42-43.

[331] Bodil Hjerrild, *Zoroastrian Divorce* (Leiden: Brill, 1988), 71.

his wife in marriage to a Zoroastrian man who cannot marry due to poverty.[332] The religious

texts promoted the practice as charity and gift to a co-religionist.[333] Mazaheri believes, in

practice, the husband may give his old or barren wife up to a co-religious man whose wife is

dead and whose children need to be taken care of.[334] Mazaheri's suggestion is in accordance with

implication of some passages in Dinkard. "…A wife to another man…"[335]; "A wife can be given

only to a Mazda-worshiper;"[336] "…To whom the gift of a wife…"[337] This does not refer to the

fertility of the abandoned wife. The passages merely address a husband relinquishing his wife to

another man. It is worth mentioning that the husband's power of guardianship over the principal

wife can easily lead to manipulating her, allowing the husband to get rid of his unwanted wife by

the means of religious justification and without returning her dowry or paying any kind of

divorce settlement.[338]

II. Economic Relations in Divorce

There is a passage in MHD suggesting if a wife is divorced by her consent, she may take

back the possession she brought to the marriage while her earnings through her personal efforts,

---

[332] Perikhanian, MHD, 101; Shaki, "The Sasanian Matrimonial," 337.

[333] James Darmesteter, *The Zend-Avesta, [Part 1, The Vendidad]*, Avesta, 1995, 32, accessed October 15, 2016, http://www.avesta.org/vendidad/vd_eng.pdf; Shaki, "Divorce."

[334] Mazaheri, *khanevadeh Irani,* 102-3.

[335] Sanjana, DK, Book 9, Bag Nask, Fargard 21.

[336] Ibid., Book 8, Nigadum Nask, section 5.

[337] Ibid.

[338] It is written in Vandidad 4:44 that "If men of the same faith, either friends or brothers, come to an agreement together, that one may obtain from the other, either goods, or a wife, or knowledge, let him who desires goods have them delivered to him; let him who desires a wife receive and wed her; let him who desires knowledge be taught the holy word [manthra spenta]."

the property that the husband gave her, or the earnings she generated through her capital

investment, are not reversible and remain with the husband.[339]

> Some have said that everything brought (by her) in connection with the marriage – such
> as, for instance, (her) paraphernalia and (her) dowry shall be taken away by her, but that
> which was acquired during the marriage shall remain.[340]

> The wife is not entitled to take ("does not take away") the property conveyed to her by
> her husband during the marriage if he dissolves the marriage with her consent, and it (=
> the property) remains with the husband.[341]

Divorce based on the wife's guilt should be rare, since it needed proof. And in such

cases, she would receive nothing and be worthy of death. However, in REA there is one passage

that states an innocent wife who has been divorced against her will, "on the death of her husband

the property held by her passes to the family of the husband." The family of the husband is still

responsible for her livelihood: food, cloths, shelter and the like.[342] Even if a wife accepts the new

husband to whom her principal husband handed her over, she cannot take back her own property

from the principal husband. According to MHD,

> A man is entitled to hand over his wife from a principal marriage, without the wife's
> consent to a man bereft of wife and children and innocent of this bereavement, who has
> legally (officially) requested a wife. And if he hands her over, then the wife's property
> does not go to the one to whom he conveyed his wife.[343]

---

[339] Reading major works in the field of the Sasanian family law, I have not seen any
doubt regarding the right of the divorcee to take back her dowry, certainly based on this passage
of MHD, however, I believe, using the word "some have said" means otherwise was the norm.

[340] Perikhanian, MHD, 35.

[341] Ibid.

[342] Safa-Isfehani, REA, 51; Shaki, "Divorce."

[343] Perikhanian, MHD, 101.

The above quote from MHD 4, 11-13 begins with "some have said," meaning it was not such a solid rule that in time of divorce the dowry should transfer to the wife. In my opinion, what is written in MHD is just some jurists' opinion or at the most a descriptive norm rather than a supportive social norm. It is not far from assumption that the divorcee wife was not given any possession unless she had a powerful paternal family.

Islamic Divorce

A remarkable aspect of Muslim divorce is its extensive association with the Quranic verses. The Quran has many regulations about dissolution of marriage as well as rulings against some sort of domestic violence against the wife that may lead to a compulsory divorce. Articulating Islamic divorce law was subject to numerous debates amongst scholars since the 1st century AH, yet like other parts of the Islamic jurisprudence, it too continued to change and adjust along with the social, political, and economic changes in Muslim majority societies. The gradual changes in law regarding wife's rights in divorce were far more radical than marriage law and regulations, as we will find later.

Here I examine different types of dissolution of marriage in the Islamic tradition that prevailed in early Islamic societies, mainly in Mesopotamia before the establishment of the jurisprudential schools in third and forth century AH to the end of the Umayyad dynasty and early Abbasid period. Muslim jurists have elaborated on the Islamic law in great detail; yet, fulfilling the purpose of this thesis does not require discussing every rule in detail. In Islamic family law, divorce was associated with regular marriage, both with a free woman or slave girl, since temporary marriage and concubinage do not need divorce in order to be terminated.

I. Elements and Unique Aspects of Islamic Divorce

Islamic divorce, like marriage, has some essential elements, which may differ slightly in each jurisprudential school. Broadly speaking, a verbal statement or formula, a husband who is mature and sane with an intention to divorce his wife, and a legal wife in a permissible stage for divorce are the pillars for legal divorce.[344] The husband should be rational and willing to divorce his wife thus a divorce under coercion is not valid.[345] A wife cannot be divorced when she is in conditions such as menstruation or birth confinement. Unlike Sunnite schools, the twelvers consider the presence of two male witnesses a pillar and mandatory.[346]

Waiting period, ***idda.*** *Idda* is a waiting period between the time of the dissolution of a marriage and the time that the wife can remarry. The rule has been rooted in the Quranic verses, which have instructed the divorcee to wait three months and ten days after the divorce in case she wants to remarry and the widow to wait four months and ten days to do so. However, those certain times can be adjusted by pregnancy and menstruation, since the waiting period has been established to make sure whether the wife is pregnant and to identify the real father of the potential child. Furthermore, *idda* gives the husband who divorced his wife over other candidates a chance/privilege to return to her under the same marriage contract. Relevant verses include Quran: 65:1-4, 2:228.

> O Prophet, when you [Muslims] divorce women, divorces them for [the commencement of] their waiting period and keep count of the waiting period, and fear Allah, your Lord. Do not turn them out of their houses, nor should they leave unless they are committing a clear immorality. And those are the limits [set by] Allah. And whoever transgresses the

---

[344] Spectorsky, *Chapters in Marriage and Divorce*, 27-28.

[345] Ibid., 36.

[346] Murata, "*Mut'a.*"

limits of Allah has certainly wronged himself. You know not; perhaps Allah will bring about after that a [different] matter.

And when they have [nearly] fulfilled their term, either retain them according to acceptable terms or part with them according to acceptable terms. And bring to witness two just men from among you and establish the testimony for [the acceptance of] Allah. That is instructed to whoever should believe in Allah and the Last day. And whoever fears Allah - He will make for him a way out.[347]

Revocable and irrevocable divorce. Islamic tradition remembers divorce as the most unpleasing, yet, permitted act in the sight of God. (Abu Dawud, Hadith 1863, Ibn Majah, Hadith 2008). In terms of avoiding divorce, one of the Quranic schemes allows the couple to reconcile without a new marriage contract during the duration of *idda*. According to the Quran,

> And when ye have divorced women and they reach their term, place not difficulties in the way of their marrying their husbands if it is agreed between them in kindness. This is an admonition for him among you who believeth in Allah and the Last Day. That is more virtuous for you, and cleaner. Allah knoweth; ye know not.[348]

However, Muslim jurists indicate that there are some other situations that divorce could not be revocable, for instance, in the cases when the wife initiates divorce, the husband divorces his wife for the third time, and the husband divorces his wife before the consummation of their marriage.[349]

> O You who have believed, when you marry believing women and then divorce them before you have touched them, then there is not for you any waiting period to count concerning them. So provide for them and give them a gracious release.[350]

---

[347] Quran, 65:1-2.

[348] Quran, 2:232.

[349] Spectorsky, *Chapters in Marriage and Divorce*, 105, 108.

[350] Quran, 33:49.

II. Types of Dissolution of a Marriage

Dissolution of a marriage could be unilateral or consensual; unilateral divorce could be revocable in which the couple can reconcile under the terms of the original marriage contract during a specified waiting period, *idda*; or irrevocable, in which the divorce is final.[351] There were four basic late antique[352] Islamic divorce practices. First, the husband divorces his wife and pays her dower or any divorce settlement. Secondly, the husband offers his wife the option of choosing divorce or staying with him; if she chooses divorce, he pays her the full divorce settlement. Third, the wife divorces her husband and she pays some form of divorce settlement by relinquishing part or all of her dower. Finally, a court divorces a couple because of a variety of reasons,[353] which will come in the following.

Regular divorce. In spite of some matriarchal background to Arabian societies, it became mostly patriarchal toward the advent of Islam. The prevailing custom in patriarchal societies for dissolution of a marriage was to place it in the hand of the husband. The custom continued in the Islamic era with some Quranic modifications. The regular and most prevailing Islamic divorce is unilateral and reversible -- one that allows the husband to divorce his wife whenever he desires by paying a specific compensations, dowry, dower or some other divorce settlement. About a proper revocable divorce, Spectorsky writes:

> A man who wishes to divorce his wife should do so at the end of her menstrual periods without resuming sexual relations with her. His wife then begins to wait an *idda* (waiting period before she can marries someone else), to ascertain whether she is pregnant. Her *idda* lasts three menstrual cycles, or three months if she does not menstruate due to age or

---

[351] Ali, *Marriage and Slavery*, 84.

[352] This classification comes by Lena Salayma for the time period between 610-750 CE.

[353] Lena Salayma, *The Beginnings of Islamic Law: Late Antique Islamicate Legal Traditions* (Cambridge: Cambridge University Press, 2016), 174-75.

illness. If she is pregnant, her delivery ends her *idda*. At any time during a woman's *idda* her husband is free to return to her. Once her *idda* has ended, she is divorced from her husband.[354]

The terms that the Quranic verses have indicated for divorce include kindness and

generosity toward the divorcee, the possibility of reversion to marriage, and maintaining the

wife's financial matters. In case of divorce, the bride retains her marriage portion:

> O Prophet, when you [Muslims] divorce women, divorce them for [the commencement of] their waiting period and keep count of the waiting period, and fear Allah, your Lord. Do not turn them out of their [husbands'] houses, nor should they [themselves] leave [during that period] unless they are committing a clear immorality. And those are the limits [set by] Allah. And whoever transgresses the limits of Allah has certainly wronged himself. You know not; perhaps Allah will bring about after that a [different] matter.[355]

> And when you divorce women and they have [nearly] fulfilled their term, either retain them according to acceptable terms or release them according to acceptable terms, and do not keep them, intending harm, to transgress [against them]. And whoever does that has certainly wronged himself. And do not take the verses of Allah in jest. And remember the favor of Allah upon you and what has been revealed to you of the Book and wisdom by which He instructs you. And fear Allah and know that Allah is Knowing of all things.[356]

> And when you divorce women and they have fulfilled their term, do not prevent them from remarrying their [former] husbands if they agree among themselves on an acceptable basis. That is instructed to whoever of you believes in Allah and the Last Day. That is better for you and purer, and Allah knows and you know not.[357]

Based on the Quranic verses, even though the marriage was not consummated, the

husband has to pay some compensation, whether a divorce settlement had been appointed:

> And if you divorce them before you have touched them and you have already specified for them an obligation, then [give] half of what you specified - unless they forego the right or the one in whose hand is the marriage contract foregoes it. And to forego it is

---

[354] Spectorsky, *Chapters in Marriage and Divorce,* 27-28.

[355] Quran, 65:1.

[356] Quran, 2: 231.

[357] Quran, 2: 232.

nearer to righteousness. And do not forget graciousness between you. Indeed Allah, of whatever you do, is Seeing.[358]

There is no blame upon you if you divorce women you have not touched nor specified for them an obligation. But give them [a gift of] compensation – the wealthy according to his capability and the poor according to his capability - a provision according to what is acceptable, a duty upon the doers of good.[359]

Takhyir.

O Prophet, say to your wives, "If you should desire the worldly life and its adornment, then come, I will provide for you and give you a gracious release.
But if you should desire Allah and His Messenger and the home of the Hereafter – then indeed, Allah has prepared for the doers of good among you a great reward."[360]

An incident of spousal conflict in the prophet's household,[361] followed by the prophet's abandonment of his wives for twenty-nine days, ended up in the revelation of the above verses, with the prophet ordered by God to offer his rebellious and unhappy wives two choices. Based on Muslim jurists' interpretations of the verses 33:28-29, as a divine order to the prophet that also should be followed by believers, early Muslim scholars added a jurisprudential topic to their divorce chapter, *Takhyir*, in which a husband give his wife a "choice" to divorce him. The verse simply instructs the prophet, in case his wives do not desire to stay with him, to grant them a gracious divorce – meaning, the prophet does not have the right to keep his wives in an undesired marriage. For Muslim women, it clearly means God granted women the right of dissolution of their unwanted marriage.

---

[358] Quran, 2: 237.

[359] Quran, 2: 236.

[360] Quran, 33: 28-29.

[361] Nabia Abbott, *Aisha, the Beloved of Mohammed* (Chicago: University of Chicago Press, 1944), 51-56.

However, the Muslim scholars had a hard time applying this Quranic statement into the jurisprudential ruling without blemishing the husband's power and control over his matrimonial affairs.[362] For instance, they restricted the implication of the verses by adding conditions: the wife should make her choice "right then and there, when her husband offers.[363] Shi'a scholars rely on a *hadith* from their sixth *Imam* proclaiming that even if the wife made her choice it does not mean divorce. It is still the husband's choice whether to divorce her or not.[364]

Wife-initiated divorce, *khul.* Esposito believes that in patriarchal pre-Islamic times, a wife had no right to divorce her husband, and it was the Quran that granted her "some judicial relief" from an unwanted marriage."[365] Lapidus in his history argues, even though "the Quran tried to prevent hasty and willful divorces by urging delay, reconciliation, and mediation by families," however, "prophetic practice indicates that women also had the right to initiate divorce."[366]

The verse associated with the wife-initiated divorce in the Quran is 2:229,

> It is not lawful for you that ye take from women aught of that which ye have given them; except (in the case) when both fear that they may not be able to keep within the limits (imposed by) Allah. And if ye fear that they may not be able to keep the limits of Allah, in that case it is no sin for either of them if the woman ransoms herself. These are the limits (imposed by) Allah.

---

[362] Scott C. Lucas, "Divorce, Hadith-Scholar Style: From al-Darimi to al-Tirmidhi," *Journal of Islamic Studies* 19, no. 3 (2008): 338-9.

[363] Spectorsky, *Chapters in Marriage and Divorce*, 48.

[364] Tabatabaee, *al-Mizan*, 33: 28-35.

[365] John L. Esposito, and Natana J. DeLong-Bas, *Women in Muslim Family Law* (Syracuse, NY: Syracuse University Press, 2004), 30.

[366] Lapidus, *Islamic Societies*, 184.

The verse has an "occasion of revelation" story in which the prophet approved a woman divorcing her husband by returning her marriage portion. The *hadith* is reported in earliest *hadith* collections, including, Abd al-Razzagh al-Sana'ni and Ibn Abi Shayba as well as the major later canonical texts. The Arabic word for wife-initiated divorce is *khul*, meaning to pull off, to cast off.[367] There is historical evidence that indicate it is practiced by the time of four successors of the prophet (*caliphs*). Ibn Abi Shaybah narrates "Umar (d. 644), the second caliph, condemned criticism of women who demanded a divorce by forfeiting their dowers. This type of criticism is apparent in reports that women who pursue forfeiture divorces are morally compromised."[368]

Wife-initiated divorce has been gradually restricted through the process of the development of legal schools; Esposito states, "the strong influence of social customs … succeeded in limiting that relief to very narrow grounds."[369] Therefore, wife-initiated divorce, which was associated with relinquishing part of, or the entire, dower in the early period, became a husband's right to divorce his wife without paying any divorce settlement. In her investigation regarding the history of wife-initiated divorce, Salayma illustrates how the term *khul*, which had been used for wife-initiated divorce in an earlier period, became a term used for a type of divorce in which the husband paid less than the full divorce settlement. Salayma writes,[370]

> This historical evidence unambiguously records a wife's ability to initiate and to affect a divorce (*khul*) in seventh-century [C.E.] Arabia, but the conditions surrounding a wife's divorce option were imprecise. ... Professional jurists replaced the imprecision

---

[367] Spectorsky, *Chapters in Marriage and Divorce*, 50.

[368] Salayma, *The Beginnings of Islamic Law*, 174.

[369] Esposito, *Women in Muslim Family Law*, 30.

[370] For a brief and informative account of the gradual decline of wife-initiated divorce see Lena Salayma, "Every law tells a story: orthodox divorce in Jewish and Islamic legal histories," *UC Irvine Law Review* 4, no.1 (2014): 19-63.

surrounding wife-initiated divorce with elaborate juridical categories. In comparison to earlier *hadith* collections (*musannafat*), slightly later, canonical compilations reduce the number of reports about wife-initiated divorce (*khul*) and limit these divorces to situations where a wife has "sufficient" grounds.[371]

Nevertheless, late antique jurists ruled that if a husband abuses his wife in order to pressure her to pursue a forfeiture divorce, then that divorce is void and the wife receives her full dower unless the wife commits an obvious sin. The rule had been affected by the Quran 4:19, "Do not compel them (women) to give away part of what you have given them unless they commit an obvious sin." While there was a continuing debate regarding revocable or irrevocable nature of *khul,* yet it has mostly been considered an irrevocable dissolution of marriage.

Divorce by court order. There was and still is a way that a wife could ask for dissolution of her marriage without partially relinquishing her dower or negotiating her husband's consent. According to Islamic Law, dissolution of a marriage may happen when a spouse suffers from "physical or mental causes that make the continuation of marriage relationships difficult or impossible, such as insanity, emasculation, and impotence for men and insanity, leprosy, a blocked vagina, and blindness for women. A spouse with grounds for annulment goes to a religious judge, who issues a formal statement.[372]

---

[371] Salayma, *The Beginnings of Islamic Law*, 175.

[372] Sachiko Murata, "Divorce: In the Shi'ite Law," in *Encyclopedia Iranica,* 1995, accessed October 15, 2016, http://www.iranicaonline.org/articles/divorce#pt3.

II. Domestic Violence and Divorce: Specific Wife-Harassment Acts That May End Union or Reunion.

There are repeated voices in the verses of the Quran that forbid the husband from hurting his wife at the time of discord and conflict. Violating these Quranic rulings could be followed by compensation and may lead to divorce. Thus it is so for repeatedly divorcing her and taking her back, stopping marital relations without divorcing her, or accusing her for adultery without sufficient ground. The Quranic statements regarding these subjects have been entered in *hadith* collections and jurisprudence as *Zihar, ila and li'an* as well as the necessity of a 'mediator' when a man already has three times divorced his wife.

Zihar. Zihar was a custom in Arabia before Islam; when a man who had conflict with his wife might swear, "you are for me as the back of my mother,"[373] which means you and I are like siblings. In fact, by this statement he ended sexual relations with her. In that way he abandoned his wife yet did not let her enter into another marriage. This would be considered a kind of domestic violence in which the sexual right of the wife is transgressed. The Quranic verses condemned the act and regulated its consequences. According to the Quran,

> Those who pronounce *zihar* among you [to separate] from their wives – they are not [consequently] their mothers. Their mothers are none but those who gave birth to them. And indeed, they are saying an objectionable statement and a falsehood. But indeed, Allah is Pardoning and Forgiving.[374]

> Allah has not made for a man two hearts in his interior. And He has not made your wives whom you declare unlawful your mothers. And he has not made your adopted sons your [true] sons. That is [merely] your saying by your mouths, but Allah says the truth, and He guides to the [right] way.[375]

---

[373] Spectorsky, *Chapters in Marriage and Divorce*, 39.

[374] Quran, 58:2.

[375] Quran, 33:4.

Here the husband has two options, either divorce his wife or pay compensation and go back to her.[376]

> And those who pronounce *zihar* from their wives and then [wish to] go back on what they said – then [there must be] the freeing of a slave before they touch one another. That is what you are admonished thereby; and Allah is Acquainted with what you do.

> And he who does not find [a slave] – then a fast for two months consecutively before they touch one another; and he who is unable – then the feeding of sixty poor persons. That is for you to believe [completely] in Allah and His Messenger; and those are the limits [set by] Allah. And for the disbelievers is a painful punishment.[377]

Ila. Based on the Quran 2:226-27 Muslim jurists regulated law against the act of *ila*, an oath taken by the husband that he would not have sex with his wife:

> For those who swear not to have sexual relations with their wives is a waiting time of four months, but if they return [to normal relations] – then indeed, Allah is Forgiving and Merciful. And if they decide on divorce – then indeed, Allah is Hearing and Merciful.

The Quranic verses indicate the husband should either divorce his wife or go back to her, within four months. Even though the Quran does not go any further, however the jurists discussed "the details of the procedures a man should follow in order to expiate his oath and resume sexual relations with his wife."[378]

Sworn allegation, *li'an*. If a husband is sure that his wife committed adultery or the child, whom she is pregnant with, does not belong to him and he is also unable to collect four witnesses, he cannot commit violence against her. The Quranic solution is what jurisprudence

---

[376] Spectorsky, *Women in Classical Islamic Law,* 134-35.

[377] Quran, 58:3,4.

[378] Spectorsky, *Women in Classical Islamic Law,* 141.

named *Li'an,* a procedure in which husband and wife swear to God that they would tell the truth

and God's curse be upon the liar.[379] According to the Quran 24:6-10,

> And those who accuse their wives [of adultery] and have no witnesses except themselves
> – then the witness of one of them [shall be] four testimonies [swearing] by Allah that
> indeed, he is of the truthful. And the fifth [oath will be] that the curse of Allah be upon
> him if he should be among the liars. But, it will prevent punishment from her if she gives
> four testimonies [swearing] by Allah that indeed, he is of the liars. And the fifth [oath
> will be] that the wrath of Allah be upon her if he was of the truthful. And if not for the
> favor of Allah upon you and His mercy... and because Allah is Accepting of repentance
> and Wise.

After the procedure, the couple was considered divorced. The Quran is silent about what should

happen next, however, the jurists made a considerable amount of debates regarding the details;

for example, the presumptive child goes to the whom or whether the couple can remarry.[380]

Triple divorce. According to the Quran a man can only divorce his wife twice; if he

divorces her for the third time, he can neither return to her during her *idda* nor marry her after

idda on a new marriage contract, unless she first fully marries another man and separates from

the latter husband by his death or divorce, then the former husband can marry her again with a

new marriage contract.

> Divorce is twice. Then, either keep [her] in an acceptable manner or release [her] with
> good treatment. And it is not lawful for you to take anything of what you have given
> them unless both fear that they will not be able to keep [within] the limits of Allah. But if
> you fear that they will not keep [within] the limits of Allah, then there is no blame upon
> either of them concerning that by which she ransoms herself. These are the limits of
> Allah; so do not transgress them. And whoever transgresses the limits of Allah - it is
> those who are the wrong doers.[381]

---

[379] For a brief account of early jurists' discussions about *Li'an* see (Lucas, 340-44).

[380] Esposito, *Women in Muslim Family Law,* 34-35; Spectorsky, *Women in Classical Islamic Law*, 128-29.

[381] Quran, 2:229.

And if he has divorced her [for the third time], then she is not lawful to him afterward until [after] she marries a husband other than him. And if the latter husband divorces her [or dies], there is no blame upon the woman and her former husband for returning to each other if they think that they can keep [within] the limits of Allah. These are the limits of Allah, which He makes clear to a people who know.[382]

The verses caused the invention of a type of divorce with specific characteristics and rulings, three divorces in one occasion: an irrevocable divorce that needs a "mediator" if the husband wants to remarry his divorcee wife. Muslim jurists have discussed the issue extensively and by details, beyond the scope of this paper.[383]

III. Financial Relations in Divorce

A divorcee wife should remain in her husband's home until the end of her *idda*.[384] She is entitled to a marriage portion or divorce settlement. She might relinquish her dower or part of it if she initiated the divorce, if she inherited from her husband during his terminal illness if he divorced her,[385] or if he died before the end of her *idda*. A divorcee was heir to her children if she survived them. On the rights of a triply divorced wife during her *idda*, in his comparative study of the "Book on divorce in the major third/ninth-century Sunni *hadith* collections," Lucas illustrates how early scholars took radically different approaches. For instance, in some *hadiths*, the divorced woman receives both lodging and maintenance while in others she receives neither

---

[382] Quran, 2:230.

[383] Spectorsky, *Chapters in Marriage and Divorce*, 29, 164.

[384] Quran, 65:1.

[385] Spectorsky, *Chapters in Marriage and Divorce*, 118.

lodging nor maintenance; also in some *hadiths* she receives lodging but does not receive maintenance.[386]

Divorce Law: Common Elements and Quranic Interference

The husband's practical unilateral right of divorce is perhaps the immediate resemblance of divorce in those traditions. While in the Islamic tradition there are no restrictions on the husband's right to divorce his wife, in Zoroastrianism, divorce takes place only with the wife's consent. However, practically, there was a way that a husband not only could divorce his wife without her consent, he also did not have to return her dowry or pay any divorce settlement. For instance, he could simply enter her into an auxiliary marriage with a poor man who was in want of such cheap cohabit, since the auxiliary wife did not need a "bride price" and could be paid nothing.

In Islamic traditions, considering the facts that the payment of dower was paid to the wife at the beginning of the marriage[387] and the bride's family did not have to pay her inheritance, as her dowry, to her husband's family in the beginning of marriage, then at the time of divorce the husband did not owe her much. However, in a few centuries after the prophet, the jurisprudential activities manipulated the divorce procedure, in which wife-initiated divorce became a kind of divorce by court or divorce with the consent of the husband, in which a husband can divorce his wife but does not have to pay her dower in full or at all.[388]

---

[386] Lucas, "Divorce, Hadith-Scholar Style," 335.

[387] The practice later changed so the dower was "partially paid at the contract formation and the remainder was recorded as a kind of debt the husband's estate owed the wife, due at divorce or at his death." Salayma, "Every Law Tells a Story," 40.

[388] Salayma, *The Beginnings of Islamic Law*, 175-76.

The extensive contribution of Quranic verses to Islamic divorce procedure made it distinct from older traditions' regular divorce. However after a few centuries, the juridical elaborations changed the divorce options to something very similar to other patriarchal legal systems of the ancient world. For example, Salayma illustrates how this early period of Islamic divorce law impacted rabbinic tradition, before both traditions limited wife-initiated divorce remarkably. She writes,

> According to the orthodox story, in the Geonic period (620-1050 CE), the rabbis felt "pressured" by the influence of Islamic courts to change existing practices by facilitating a no-fault divorce option for women. In the era of the Rishonim (1050-1400 CE), the rabbis corrected the "deviant: Geonic practice and returned Jewish law to its "original" foundations by prohibiting women from no-fault divorce.[389]

Nevertheless, for a Sasanian/Zoroastrian wife like her Muslim sister, there was many social and cultural obstacles to initiate a divorce that made divorce just a possibility for the small group of very wealthy and powerful families who actually could protect their divorcee daughter from those social and cultural hardships.

Investigating divorce regulations, a common concern about an innocent wife whose husband divorced her during his terminal illness in Muslim and Zoroastrian communities seems noticeable. Spectorsky reports, By the second/eighth century some new ruling held that if a terminally ill man divorces his wife/wives, likely because deprives her from inheritance, and die from the illness, the divorce is invalid and the wife inherits from him.[390] Zoroastrian text of forth/tenth century Iran, REA answer 7, held that an innocent principal wife who "does not agree to such unjust divorce, … should remain principal wife," whether her husband is alive or has

---

[389] Ibid., 180.

[390] Spectorsky, *Women in Classical Islamic Law,* 118.

passed away.[391] Apparently, if the husband would remain alive, he could get rid of an unwanted

wife without paying any compensation; the significance of the ruling is that divorcee could

inherent from her dead husband, similar to the Muslim regulations. Observing the time of

Muslim and Zoroastrian documents, in this case, the adoption of idea is seemingly in reverse.

---

[391] Safa-Isfehani, REA, 51.

CHAPTER 5

CONCLUSION

Countries with majority Muslim populations have elements of classical Muslim family law in their personal status codes and civil law, articulated in the classical period of the formation of Islamic Law more than a thousand years ago. Muslim family law contains numerous gender inequalities such as inequality embodied in Muslim marriage and divorce regulations: polygamy; husband's right of unilateral divorce; wife's restrictions to initiate divorce; and the lack of legal access to the family's asset, which is usually under the name of the husband; as well as the necessity of the presence of a male guardian for the purpose of marrying off the bride.

During the establishment of Islam as an institution, the recently converted Muslims, who had been comfortable with their previous long-lasting patriarchal family order as a decent way of life, proclaimed that the full control of male over female was a divine order. Yet they could not find a clear Quranic statement, especially in the field of sexuality and marriage, which would confirm their family order in details. As a result, male Muslim scholars facilitated jurisprudence and Quranic exegesis to articulate family law, neglecting and nullifying the verses that could be interpreted in favor of the rights of the Muslim woman. For instance, the Quran assigned women a right to obtain possessions as a result of their own work, inheritance and marriage portion, and these possessions gave them a degree of independence; however jurisprudential rules tried to regain control over women's professional development and business activities by legislating the necessity of the husband's permission for a wife to leave the house.

The Abbasid Empire had been established in the old territory of Sasanian Empire. It is a universally accepted idea that the cultures and religious traditions influence one another once they are in contact. Geoffrey Partington, in his book *Making Sense of History,* writes,

> Usually conquerors impose their historical and cultural traditions on the defeated, but there are many example of the reverse process. Nomadic peoples who conquered the kingdoms of Mesopotamia typically adopted the way of life of the fertile plains within two generations.[392]

Seemingly, the reverse adoption process took place after the conquest of the Sasanian Empire by the Arabs. The Abbasid Empire adapted numerous aspects of the Persian Sasanian Empire. Furthermore, the formation of the Islamic jurisprudence happened during the first couple centuries of the Abbasid era, mostly by Persian-descendant scholars and within the land that the Sasanian civilization and their "higher culture" had prevailed.

The process is more likely to be accurate in the case of family law, since family law is usually the most conservative and long-lasting part of a culture. The Islamic family law certainly did reject part of the Zoroastrian family law, mostly due to the Quran's straightforward statement against them. For instance, the incestuous marriage or the Sasanian inheritance law has been rejected; but clearly the rest has been absorbed. I believe that despite the apparent differences between the two religions of Zoroastrianism and Islam, there are numerous resemblances in their marriage customs and family law.

Although a lack of enough relevant sources, mainly related to the first century of the Islamic era, does not allow an indisputable conclusion, the similarities of an ideal marital relations in terms of mutual duties as well as the definition of a pious wife in Zoroastrianism and Islam could be observed as a sign of cultural continuity in the region.

---

[392] Geoffrey Partington, *Making Sense of History* (Bloomington, IN: Xlibris, 2013), 27.

The widespread type of marriage in Islam shares the same elements of the principal marriage of the Sasanian period. The notions such as guardianship, joined duty of wife's obedience vs. husband's maintenance, the necessity of the bride's virginity, the importance of being within same social rank, the presence of witnesses, the same order of offers/acceptances as well as many other cultural and juridical similarities beyond the limitations of this paper. Considering these facts, I intend to imply that the claims regarding the sacred roots of the Islamic family law are controversial and questionable.

Limited academic work has been done on the impact of Zoroastrianism on early Islamic culture and creeds. However, much more can be done. For instance, comparative inquiries may illustrate how a number of Muslim jurisprudential rules pertaining to women resemble those of the Zoroastrians. Some of these rulings may be easily proven to be incompatible with the Quranic *Weltanschauung* and even the literal meanings of relevant verses. As a result, the distance between the teachings of the Quran, as the most legitimate/authentic Islamic sources, and Muslim jurisprudential rules would mostly reject, as divinely sourced, gender inequality legalized by *Sharia*.

The impact of Iranian culture and religion was not limited to jurisprudence, yet in maxims and religious stories ascribed to the prophet and his companions we are witnessing the traces of Iranian old traditions. Shaul Shaked in his article "Hadith as Influenced by Iranian Ideas and Practices," argues, "The body of *hadith* contains evidence of various kinds for the contacts of the Islamic community in the early centuries of its history with Persians and Zoroastrian notions."[393] Shaked recounts some of these records, however, he confirms, "no monographic

---

[393] Shaul Shaked, "Hadith as Influenced by Iranian Ideas and Practices," in *Encyclopedia Iranica*, accessed October 15, 2016, http://www.iranicaonline.org/articles/hadith-v.

work on this subject has yet appeared."[394] There are numerous similarities between Muslim and

Zoroastrian literature regarding women and womanhood, which can be the subject of both

academic inquiry and gender equality debates. For instance, the Zoroastrian image of "female"

can be traced in the *hadith* collections as well. In this work, I illustrated how a maxim ascribed to

Aisha has resemblance to a saying in MHD. In my article, "Women's Afterlife Punishment: the

Roots of Islamic Divine Comedy," I illustrate how a narration regarding sins and punishments of

a female sinner in hell and how even the format of those narrations in these two Zoroastrian and

Muslim texts of *Ard□Wir□z-N□mag*[395] and *Uyun Akhbar-e-Reda*[396] respectively, are almost

identical. *The Book of Ard□Wir□z-N□mag* is a Zoroastrian description of Heaven, Limbo and

Hell, and the book of *Oyun Akhbar Reda* is a Shi'a collection of *hadith*, which was written by

prominent Iranian Shi'a scholar of forth/tenth century, Ibn B□bawayh Al-Qumm□, known as

Shaikh e. Sadoogh. Al-Qummi, resided in Qom, one of the oldest Shi'a population centers in

Iran.[397]

Another challenging subject regarding female body is menstrual period, which was the

subject of many researches in the Zoroastrian studies. Dryaee writes,

---

[394] Ibid.

[395] Wahman, Far□d□n. *Arda Wir□z N□mag: The Iranian "Divina Commedia"* (London:
Curzon Press, 1986).

[396] Mu□ammad Ibn □Al□Ibn B□bawayh Al-Qumm□, *Source of Traditions on Imam Reza =
Oyun Akhbar Al-Reza* (Qum: Ansariyan, 2006).

[397] After examining two narrations, I concluded, "Looking at these texts, the causes and
the means of punishments are fairly similar. Given the similarities in sins and punishments, these
two traditions follow the same perceptual structure of a righteous woman, an obedient, inferior,
and absolutely trustee of the husband's interests. On the other hand the Quran does admit neither
the sins nor the punishments regarding those sins in its text."

Laws forbidding women from taking part in daily activity, such as cooking, cleaning and
coming into contact with the sacred fire during the time of menstruation are detailed and
abundant. Women who engaged in intercourse during the period of menstruation were
worthy of death. Men were to avoid women during their menstrual period, because this
was the time when women were seen as most contagious and dangerous to every living
being. According to the *Vandidad* they had to be kept in an enclosure where they would
not be seen until their menstruation cycle was over.[398]

On the other hand, there is little evidence regarding female impurity during the monthly period in

the Quran; there is no specific Quranic ruling that indicates fasting is prohibited during menses.

The Quran did specify the causes that exempt a person from fasting yet menstruation was not

among them; furthermore there are no Quranic evidences that a menses woman should not pray

or attend a mosque. Nevertheless, Muslim scholars and jurists have imposed these and many

other rulings on the lives of the Muslim women; all of these kinds of discrepancies could be

subjects for future studies, since the Quran can be read as an egalitarian sacred text.

Access to women's sexuality in Zoroastrian/Sasanian tradition and Islamic tradition has

no limitations except in the case of a married woman; the rest depended on the man's social and

financial abilities. Male jurisprudential activities in both traditions just served patriarchy and

male sexual desire and comfort. On the other hand, the original teachings of the prophet of Islam

attempted to limit sexual activities within the legal boundaries that would have maintained a

limited economic and social security for women.

---

[398] Daryaee, *Sasanian Persia*, 99.